MW01612287

WHO NEEDS ME?
THE CHRISTIAN ANSWER FOR GRIEF

Rev. Art E. Christmas

Infinity Publishing

Copyright © 2003 by Arthur Ewing Christmas

ISBN 0-7414-1461-9

Published by:

PUBLISHING.COM

519 West Lancaster Avenue
Haverford, PA 19041-1413
Info@buybooksontheweb.com
www.buybooksontheweb.com
Toll-free (877) BUY BOOK
Local Phone (610) 520-2500
Fax (610) 519-0261

Printed in the United States of America

Printed on Recycled Paper

Published April 2003

ACKNOWLEDGEMENTS

Many people have impacted my life over the years and taught me what I know about the subject of grief. Grief is a sacred journey. Done right, it will be a spiritual journey. I have had the sacred honor of walking with many people through the valley of the shadow of death. I am indebted to each person who has invited me into their circle of sorrow. Their names are too numerous to mention.

My special thanks go to a small group that made up a grief support group at the North Park Baptist Church of Evansville, Indiana. They were some of my main teachers and the inspiration behind this book.

My thanks go to Amy Tankersley, Ella Shelton and Ruby Rusk for the editorial work they did to iron out my many mistakes. I especially thank my wife, Dixie, for thirty-eight years of companionship. Her encouragement in this endeavor helped make it a reality.

I dedicate this book in memory of Arthur Christmas, Sr. (1915-2002) He was my father, role model and friend.

For the sake of simplicity, I have used the term "him" or "his" to be gender inclusive. I ask for your understanding in this matter.

My prayer is that this book may be helpful to those who are dealing with the pain of grief and those who are reaching out to others in their loss.

TABLE OF CONTENTS

INTRODUCTION

Of all the problems human beings face, grief and the loss of a loved one are probably the most universal and the most difficult. Jane had her story.

I was told that Jane had some real problems. I went to visit her in her home. The previous Sunday she attended our church. I had never met her, but as we sat together in her living room, her story unfolded.

She and her husband were married right out of high school. They were both eighteen years of age. Their marriage had some ups and downs, like all marriages, but the downs were very severe. He was involved with drugs. When he was high, he became violent with her. She told me how he had hurt her on several occasions: broken collarbone, black eye and broken ribs. She was in the hospital more than once.

I interrupted her to ask her why she stayed with him. She gave two reasons. She wanted to be true to her marriage vows. She could see in him the good person that he *could* be and she dreamed that he would one day become.

She continued with her story. During these violent episodes, she would pray that he would die. She was filled more with anger than fear. She *hated* him when he became physically abusive to her. Many times she prayed he would die.

At age twenty-six, her husband was diagnosed with cancer. Two years later he died. Jane was with him through all this. She loved him. Now her life was in shambles with grief. However, there was more than grief. There was guilt. She had prayed that he might die. She was stuck and couldn't move forward. Jane visited the cemetery everyday. She would go walking and end up miles from home. Grief was her bed and breakfast. Grief was her lunch and supper. How could I help?

A Spanish poet once wrote: "Traveler, there is no path; paths are made by walking". This describes the season

i

of grief. There is no road map for grief. There is no one who has walked in your shoes or can show you all you need to know. My greatest teacher was Dr. Wayne Oates. He wrote many books. One of them was called *Your Particular Grief.* The title in itself speaks volumes. Your grief is so unique. You must find your way through the pain and the hurt. You can learn from fellow travelers; but still, you must make your own path. The Scripture says: "Work out your own salvation with fear and trembling." (Philippians 2:12) I would like to substitute grief. "Work out your own grief with fear and trembling!"

The purpose of this book is to give some thoughts that can help you do the hard work of grief resolution. I have worked with people in grief over the past forty years. I do not have all the answers. No one has all the answers. Nevertheless, I hope you can glean something that will help you as you make your pathway through the jungle called grief.

EVEN JESUS TOOK TIME TO WEEP

Grief is the emotional response we experience when we suffer a loss of any kind. The more severe the loss, the more severe the grief will be. Grief that comes from severe loss touches us at the very heart of where we live, and our whole being is affected.

It is so important that we learn to be gentle and kind to ourselves at this time. This is not a normal time. This is a time of depression. To love one deeply and then to lose him is to suffer depression and deep sadness. A vacuum is left in your heart. No one else can fill a big hole that is there. One's life is changed forever and will never be the same.

To grieve you must resist the temptation to go on as usual. You may be tempted to keep a very busy schedule and thereby forget your sorrow. This will not work. Grief time must now have a real part of your schedule and your agenda. Perhaps you have given your life to your job or to your family. Perhaps you have been very thoughtful and kind to others. Now is the time to be kind and thoughtful to yourself. You will need time to be alone. You will need time to heal. It will take a great deal of time. Will you decide to be kind and gentle with yourself? Will you treat yourself with the same kindness you would offer someone else who has suffered a great loss? Even Jesus took time to weep. Will you allow yourself to do the same?

TIME HEALS ALL WOUNDS IF…

We have always heard that time heals all wounds. This is not always true. Time that heals is time that is spent in the right way. It is supremely important that we understand that grief resolution takes time, lots of time. This is so contrary to our hurried way of life. We want a quick fix. We want a ten minute band-aid. But the band-aid won't do. This is time for major surgery and a lengthy convalescent time.

Grief is an emotional reaction. We are about three-fifth emotions in our inward makeup. We are not robots. We are not automatons. We are human beings. When our very being is hurt, time slows down and we must accept this truth. If you broke your leg, you would automatically know that it was going to take time to heal. You would have it put in a cast. You would hobble around on crutches for several weeks. It would be perhaps months before your leg was back to normal. Grief resolution is similar to a broken leg...only more severe and with a longer healing process.

HOW LONG DOES IT TAKE TO HEAL?

When we suffer grief, the clock seems to stand still. The nights are long. The weeks are long. The weekends are long. The months are long. How long does it take?

One thing we must learn about grief is it leaves us with questions. It leaves us with questions that do not have an answer. How long does it take? There is no pat answer to that question. You will never get over the memories of your loved one. However, would you want to? Can you get over the pain, the deep pain and the loneliness that have been brought your way? The answer is "Yes", if you do your grief work and face your grief head-on. This takes tons of courage and faith.

The more you face your pain and deal with it correctly, the sooner the deep pain will pass on. The grandmother in the mountains of North Carolina used to say: "If you go into the big end of the horn, it will get harder and harder. If you go into the small end of the horn, it gets easier and easier."

This echoes the teachings of Jesus. "Enter through the narrow gate. For wide is the gate and broad is the road that leads to destruction, and many enter though it. But small is the gate and narrow the road that leads to life, and only a few find it." (Matthew 7:13-14. NIV)

There is no easy road to grief healing. This truth can

2

set you free. Decide now that you are not going to get in a hurry. How long does it take? It takes one day at a time.

THE SLOW WISDOM OF GRIEF

We want to refer to the "slow wisdom of grief" throughout this book. Grief, if we go through the process, can bring to us a wisdom and a perspective that helps us see more clearly what is really important in life. We learn so much more in times of sorrow than in times of pleasure. However, the lessons come slowly. We must take it easy. We must take it slowly. The writer of Ecclesiastes says, "Sorrow is better than laughter, because a sad face is good for the heart. The heart of the wise is in the house of mourning, but the heart of fools is in the house of pleasure." (Ecclesiastes 7:3,4)

Think about that for a moment. How in the world could sorrow be better than laughter? The answer is rather obvious. It is in sorrow that we dig deep into the meaning of who we are and why we are here. In your grief, learn all that you can. The more you can learn in this time of sadness, the richer you will be and the wiser you will be in the days ahead. You are inducted into the school of suffering where you get a degree in the slow wisdom of grief. Take these days very seriously. Learn all you can. You may want to keep a journal recording all your thoughts and feelings. You will not want to forget what you learn in this valley. The psalmist said, "Blessed are those whose strength is in you, who have set their hearts on pilgrimage. As they pass through the Valley of Baca, they make it a place of springs. they go from strength to strength till each appears before God in Zion." (Psalm 84:5-7.) Baca means weeping. Apply the wisdom of seeing grief as a pilgrimage. You will one day pass through this season of tears.

Remember, *this is the cost of love*. Pain is the price of love. If you did not love your departed loved one, you would not have so much pain. Therefore, see your pain in a sacred way. Is there anything more precious than love? As

3

the poet said, "'Tis better to have loved and lost than to never loved at all." One husband said of his wife that had died, "this I can do for her". He transformed his suffering to take on meaning. In marriage, one is going to be left behind unless both husband and wife die at the same time. The one left behind has the grief and loneliness with which to deal. Think of yourself as walking this lonely valley instead of his having to do it.

A phrase found throughout the scripture is "Wait upon the Lord". This is a call to slow down, to see it through over the long run and discover how the Lord will come and carry you through your pain to a new day of deeper wisdom and love.

POWERLESSNESS

Grief, as nothing else, sends us to the very depth of our being. We ask the all important questions like: who am I? Why am I here? Where am I going? What is expected of me? How can I find strength and courage for my every day responsibilities? How can I go on? These and other questions remind us of that huge feeling of powerlessness. We feel so out of control.

It is at this time that we need to remind ourselves that all power comes from God. He is the Father of compassion and the God of all comfort.(II Corinthians 1: 3) God promises to give us power if we trust in Him. "For God did not give us a spirit of timidity, but a spirit of power, of love and of self-discipline" (II Timothy 1:7)

In our weakness, if we turn to God, in time, power will replace our feelings of weakness and helplessness. "I lift up my eyes to the hills—where does my help come from? My help comes from the Lord, the Maker of heaven and earth." (Psalms 121:1,2)

Paul had a "thorn in the flesh", some physical ailment that dogged him and kept him in touch with reality. He prayed three times that this thorn would be removed. The

4

answer came back: *'My grace is sufficient for you, for my power is made perfect in weakness.'* . Paul concludes, "Therefore I will boast all the more gladly about my weaknesses, so that Christ's power may rest on me...for when I am weak, then I am strong". (II Corinthians 12:9,10)

Here is a divine paradox. When we are at our weakest, we call upon God. He gives to us a power that is greater than our own. Paul embraced his weakness. He saw it as an opportunity to know God, not a hindrance to living. Yes, by the grace of God we can make it through the valley of grief and sorrow. Millions have done it. You can too!

HITTING BOTTOM IS NO FUN

Grief takes us to the bottom of human emotions. It has been called the "dark night of the soul." You have never been lonelier. You have never been sadder. You have never been emptier. You have never been this listless and lacking of energy. This is the environment of grief. It is not a fun place to be. You can be in a large crowd and feel all alone. You can drive great distances and not get away from the hurt. It surrounds you.

Read the Psalms and you will be surprised how the writer is acquainted with you! You will ask, "How did he know how I feel?" Of course, the answer is that millions and millions have experienced what you feel. Read Psalm 13. *"How long, O Lord? Will you forget me forever? How long will you hide your face from me? How long must I wrestle with my thoughts and every day have sorrow in my heart? How long will my enemy triumph over me? Look on me and answer, O Lord my God. Give light to my eyes, or I will sleep in death."* (Psalm 13:1-3)

Sometimes we even feel that God is not hearing our prayers. We feel so all alone. One night, years ago, I had a dream. I dreamed that I was flying through space with nothing but darkness all around me. I was completely alone. I woke up in a cold sweat. Realizing it was a dream, helped me go back to sleep. But I have never forgotten that dream. And I have come to see that this is one of Jesus' description of hell. It is a place of outer darkness. (Matthew 8:12; 22:13; 25:30)It is a place of total alienation from God and from others. It is a place without companionship or communication. It is hell! Grief sometimes makes us feel that we are all alone and that God has deserted us and that no one understands what we are going through. It is no fun to be in this place.

The path through the jungle of grief must take you through the worst before you can begin to heal. You must feel your sadness. You must not run from the tears, the anger, or whatever emotions are there. You must express them. You must express them to someone else. You must express them to yourself. You must express them to God. These deep feelings of hurt will not be healed until they have been felt and expressed. Remember, you must hit bottom before you can start moving up. Don't put it off. Grief will not just evaporate with time. No! We have to wrestle with it, wade through it and work it out in our own way.

ASKING TOO MUCH, THE FAUSTIAN MISTAKE

Faust was a fictional character that traded his soul for youth, knowledge, power and pleasure. He actually was trading his soul for instant pleasure and respite from the struggles and the questions of life. It is the ancient temptation to try to avoid pain and pursue pleasure. However, this leads to slavery. Faust ends by giving his highest wisdom:

> Yes-this I hold to with devout insistence,
> Wisdom's last verdict goes to say
> He only earns both freedom and existence
> Who must reconquer them each day.

When grieving, the temptation is to avoid the pain and replace the grief with laughter and frivolity. It is a temptation which, like all temptation, must be resisted. Each

6

day one must confront the pain and the loss. Each day one must be reminded only too many times that the loved one is gone. Each day, one must reconquer the effort to find a quick fix or to make quick decisions that will take the pain away.

Albert Schweitzer, in his book *Reverence for Life*, suggests that you look back at the times in your life in which you were calm and contented and everything seemed to be going right for you. If the whole of your life had been a succession of hours like those, do you know what would have become of you? You would become selfish, hardhearted, lonely, without regard for higher things, for the pure, for God. You would never have felt blessedness. When did it first dawn on you that we don't live unto ourselves? When did the blessedness of compassion bring comfort to you? In suffering. Where did you catch a glimpse of the higher destiny of your life? In suffering. Where did you feel God was near to you? In suffering. Don't vex your mind trying to explain the suffering you have to endure in this life. Don't think that God is punishing you or disciplining you or that he has rejected you. Even in the midst of your suffering you are in his kingdom. You are always his child, and he has his protective arm around you. (Cf. *A Feast For a Time of Fasting*, Louis Cassels, pp. 70f.)

The Psalmist says *"though I walk through the valley of the shadow of death, I will fear no evil for thou art with me."* It is this "walking through" that we want to avoid. We want to "walk around" the valley and get over it. As we walk, taking no short cuts, we can reach the other side of the valley. That is our goal. *The only way out is through.* The goal is not to end the pain, but to grow through the pain.

Barbara Johnson in *Where Does A Mother Go to Resign?* tells of the slowness of working through grief and pain. Healing is a process, a daily letting go little by little.

"As children bring their broken toys,
with tears for us to mend,
     I brought my broken dreams to God,
because He was my friend.
     But then, instead of leaving Him in peace
to work along with ways
     That were my own, at last
I snatched them back and cried,
     "How can you be so slow?"
"My child," He said, "What could I do?
     You never did let go!" p. 116.

SHOCK--WHY ME?

Shock is a bigger factor in your grief if your loved one dies very suddenly. Even when we have a little time to prepare, the finality of it all leaves us with a sense of shock; almost numb and without feeling. Sometimes people are still in shock at the funeral home and while going through the funeral. It is later that the shock wears off and tears and sadness begin to flood.

Along with our shock is the persistent question of WHY? Why me? Why my child? Why my spouse? Why someone so young? Why am I the one that is left behind? Why did God allow this to happen? Questions overwhelm our soul and the questions are often left without answers. No one can answer why. We often have to live with unanswered questions.

As a teenager, an attractive young lady worked with the youth group in our church. She was a beautiful young lady. Her name was Mary Ann Logan. Mary Ann overflowed with joy and happiness. She was a senior in Medical School and was preparing to be a missionary doctor. One morning she went to the hospital to attend her classes. She held a cup of coffee in her hand as she stepped on the elevator. With one foot on and one foot off, the elevator unexpectedly jerked up, trapped her body and pinned her. She died instantly.

8

I vividly remember her funeral. To this day, forty-five years later, I do not have the answer to the question "Why?". It was tragic. It was a senseless tragedy. She was in the morning of life. How many thousands of lives would have been touched by her life in medicine? The questions remain unanswered.

The old hymn says it this way: "We will understand it better bye and bye." Jesus tells us that He will give us something better than answers to our questions. If we discovered the answer to "Why?" and received some kind of perfect explanation, would it take away the pain? No. We need something greater than an answer to all our questions. Jesus said, *"I will ask the Father, and he will give you another Counselor to be with you forever--the Spirit of truth."* (John 14:16,17)Jesus was saying that we would be given the Holy Spirit, the very presence of God to live in us forever and to give us comfort and strength. Jesus describes this presence living within us. He says, "Whoever drinks the water I give him will never thirst. Indeed, the water I give him will become in him a spring of water welling up to eternal life." (John 4:14)

We do not get an answer to all of our questions. But God promises something better...the Holy Spirit that loves, comforts and strengthens us day by day. The deep pain of our grief is healed over time as the Holy Spirit works in our hearts.

Back to our questions. They will be answered. Paul says, *"For we know in part and we prophesy in part, but when perfection comes, the imperfect disappears. Now I know in part; then I shall know fully, even as I am fully known."* (I Corinthians 13:9,10,12.) Yes, our knowledge is imperfect. We do not have all the answers now. But the day will come when our knowledge will be perfect and all of our questions will fade into insignificance. That is God's promise to us. So, in the meantime, we must thank God for His presence during all the difficult times of our lives. We can make it with His help.

EXPERIENCING THE GRACE OF GOD

Robert J. Hastings in his book *How To Help Yourself* tells the following story. Ruby Barkley Goodwin grew up in DuQuoin, an Illinois mining town about 35 miles Northwest of Marion. Her book, *It's Good to Be Black* describes small town life in DuQuoin in the years preceding World War I. Among other stories, Ruby includes one about her great grandmother Judy, a slave on an Alabama plantation. Judy's master, John Hopgood, wanted to breed her with a healthy, young buck of his choice. Judy refused to be coerced and ran off and hid in the swamps. For three years, she saw only a few brave slaves who slipped into the woods after dark to bring her bits of food and beg her to come home.

"'Taint safe, Judy. 'Taint safe for a lone woman", they warned. But Judy claimed she wasn't scared. "It the daytime I made friends with the animals. Ain't nothing wild if'en you kan talk its own talk." Then she described the nights: "The nights ain't bad neither, cause I always nowed how to talk with Jesus. But in the swamps, I done learned to let Jesus talk to me." After a few months, Mr.Hopgood called his slaves together: "If any of you all know where that old sow Judy is hiding, you can tell her to come on in. I don't aim to beat her no more but I'm selling her on down the river. Now get on back to the field."

The next morning Judy walked into the backyard of the big house. Two days later they chained her to an ox cart and marched her off to a nearby auction. But great granddaughter Ruby says Judy's head was high.

Judy learned in the depths of her pain *to let Jesus talk to her*. In the midst of your valley, you must listen closely to what Jesus is saying to you. Remember, spiritual intimacy and insight are much more available in the valley than elsewhere.

THE MIND AND THE BODY

Grief time is a time to learn to deal with depression. Grief is a normal depression. How have you dealt with depression in the past? What is it that helps lift your spirits? People everywhere are discovering the mood altering results of exercise. Exercise is not only good for your physical health, it is good for your emotional health. Exercise is time spent improving your self esteem. You may feel that you are so weak that you cannot do anything regarding physical activity. There is a paradox here. When we exercise we get more energy, not less! Find the exercise that is right for you. Notice the difference.

Then our need for a healthy diet and the temptation to eat too little or too much is often an issue to deal with during a season of grief. Job says, "I am nothing but skin and bones." (Job19:20) A loss of appetite sometimes accompanies grief. Eating alone can also be a factor in getting the right nutrition. Regardless of our circumstances, we need to take care of our bodies by eating the right kinds of food and having a healthy diet. Our body and our mind are a unity. We must be kind to ourselves physically and emotionally.

OVERLOOKING WRONG COMFORT

One of the most awkward times in life is when friends struggle to say the right thing to us in our grief. What do you say when you visit the funeral home? What do you say when you meet up with a friend that has just buried a child or a spouse or a parent? What is appropriate to say?

Sally Downham Miller tells of losing her husband to cancer at age twenty-four. She was widowed with two small children. Here husband was a teacher in the local high school and she describes three teenage girls that came to the funeral home. They had been students of her husband. They were frightened. They were hurt. They were so unacquainted with grief and death. They approached Sally and this is how she described the scene.

The first said, "Oh, Mrs. Downham, I am so sorry."

I held her hand and smiled as warmly as I could and said, "Thank you for coming."

The second stepped forward and repeated what I then realized was the rehearsed greeting, "Oh, Mrs. Downham, I am so sorry." Desiring to make it as painless as possible, I replied the same, "Thank you so much for coming."

The third, who had been watching with wide-eyed intent, took my hand as her friends had before her and said, "Oh, Mrs. Downham, thank you so much for coming." The words had no more escaped her mouth when she gasped, turned and ran out of the funeral home.

I found her heaving great sobs of embarrassment in the front yard. I took her in my arms and soothed her until she could hear me. Then I told her that her words were as good as any I'd heard that day. I, too, was uncertain about what to say and do, but I knew one thing for sure--there are no words to express the pain and bewilderment that both of us felt.(Mourning and Dancing: A Memoir of Grief and Recovery, Health Communications, Inc.; Deerfield Beach, Florida, 1999, pp. 73f.)

Of all the biblical books, the book of Job focuses the most on grief and the trauma of loss. He loses his family, his wealth and his health. Three of his friends came to comfort him. Eliphaz, Bildad and Zophar sat with Job in silence for seven days. For this we give them credit. But then they opened their mouths and started preaching sermons. They accused Job of sinning and this, according to their reasoning, was why he had met with such calamity. Job was a righteous man and he vehemently rejected this verdict. He gets angry with his friends for their words only add to his pain. He says, "You are worthless physicians, all of you! If only you would be altogether silent!" (13:4,5) He goes on to call them "miserable comforters!" (16:2)

Those of us experiencing grief have to contend with

well meaning friends who make feeble attempts at being helpful but end up being hurtful. When President Kennedy was assassinated in Dallas, Texas, we remember his wife standing by the Vice President, Lyndon Johnson as he was being sworn in as President. There on Air Force One, as Mrs. Johnson met Jacqueline Kennedy she said, "I am so sorry this happened in Dallas". Immediately she realized that she had said the wrong thing. This is easy to do. People do not know what to say. Friends often make the mistake of trying to say something and it comes out wrong.

I know a young mother who lost her only child, a thirteen-year old daughter. She was so angry at the comments that came her way that she put a sign on her door that read something like this: "Do not come in here and tell me you know how I feel. Do not come in here and tell me that I need to be thankful that I had her for thirteen years. Do not tell me that I can always have another child. Do not tell me that I can adopt another child. Do not tell me that I should be glad that my daughter is in heaven. Do not tell me that I need to get on with my life."

Harriet Sarnoff Schiff, in her excellent book, The Bereaved Parent, tells of her young son who died during an operation to correct a congenital heart malfunction. Her clergyman took her aside and said, "I know that this is a painful time for you. But I know that you will get through it all right, because God never sends us more of a burden than we can bear. God only let this happen because He knows that you are strong enough to handle it." She remembers her reaction to those words: "If only I was a weaker person, Robbie would still be alive." (Cf. *When Bad Things Happen to Good People,* Harold S. Kushner, p. 26.)

Joneta Handel speaks to the miserable comforters in this poem:

"Don't tell me that you understand,

    Don't tell me that you know.

    Don't tell me that I will survive,

    How I will surely grow.

    Don't tell me this is just a test,

    That I am truly blessed,

    That I am chosen for this task,

    Apart from all the rest.

    Don't come at me with answers

    That can only come from me,

    Don't tell me how my grief will pass

    That I will soon be free.

    Don't stand in pious judgment

    Of the bonds I must untie,

    Don't tell me how to suffer,

    And don't tell me how to cry.

    My life is filled with selfishness,

    My pain is all I see,

    But I need you; I need your love,

    Unconditionally.

    Accept me in my ups and downs

    I need someone to share,

    Just hold my hand and let me cry,

    And say, "My friend, I care."

Harold Kushner points out that it is easier to know what not to say in the face of grief and sorrow than what to say. "Anything critical of the mourner ('don't take it so hard,' 'try to hold back your tears, you're upsetting people') is wrong. Anything which tries to minimize the mourner's pain ('it's probably for the best', 'it could be a lot worse', 'she's better off now') is likely to be misguided and unappreciated. Anything which asks the mourner to disguise or reject his feelings ('we have no right to question God', 'God must love you to have selected you for this burden') is wrong as well."

Kushner goes on to give some good advice about what to say. "I feel religious people should say to those who have been hurt by life: 'This is not your fault. You are a good, decent person who deserves better. I can understand that you feel hurt, confused, angry at what happened, but there is no reason why you should feel guilty. As a man of faith, I have come here in God's name, not to judge you, but to help you. Will you let me help you?'." (*When Bad Things Happen To Good People,* pp. 89, 104)

We must learn how to cope with the miserable comforters. Some will say the wrong things at the wrong time. If only they would learn to keep their words few and encourage us to do the talking. Wisdom tells us to be quick to listen and slow to speak. (James 1:19)

If they focus on us, the bereaved, they can move from self consciousness and anxiety. They must remember why they are there. They must remember that their goal is to comfort and care for those left behind. Then in the days following the funeral, it is very important that our comforters let us know they care.

Many people refrain from talking about the deceased for fear of causing those in grief to be depressed. Just the opposite is true. We need to know that others miss our loved one also.

Terry Kettering describes the anguish that many cause the bereaved by refusing to broach the subject. After the death of his wife, Barbara, Kettering penned the following poem entitled

15

Elephant in the Room".

"There's an elephant in the room

It is large and squatting, so it is hard to get around it.

Yet, we squeeze by with "How are You?"

and "I'm fine..." and a thousand other forms of

trivial chatter.

We talk about the weather; We talk about work;

We talk about everything else...

EXCEPT THE ELEPHANT IN THE ROOM!

There's an elephant in the room,

We all know it is there.

We are thinking about the elephant as we talk.

It is constantly on our minds,

for you see, it is a very big elephant.

But we do not talk about the elephant

in the room. Oh, please say her name,

Oh, please say "Barbara" again.

Oh, please let's talk about the elephant in the room.
For if we talk about her death,

we can talk about her life.

Can I say "Barbara" and not have to look away?

For if I cannot, you are leaving me

Alone...in a room...with an elephant!"

Grief is a difficult time. It is difficult for those of us that have lost loved ones and difficult for those that would comfort us. Perhaps we can help each other understand the experience of grief.

PUT ON THE BRAKES: NO HASTY DECISIONS

When grieving, people often make hasty decisions to sell the house, the car, and everything that reminds them of their loved one. This is a mistake. It is an effort to get away from the material things that expose painful memories. It won't work. Hasty decisions won't remove the painful reminder that your loved one is gone.

One husband of fifty-eight years lost his wife, and his grown children immediately told him to sell the house and move in with them! It was their way of trying to take away the pain. They were well meaning, but this husband had the foresight to see this as a "band-aid" solution. He needed the time to grieve. He needed the time to think. He needed the time to adjust. He did not want to do anything that would be later regretted. The day might come when he would move from his home, but he put off that day and gave himself time to grieve.

Searching for a new spouse to relieve the loneliness is another hasty decision. One man met a widow one month after losing his wife. He jumped at the opportunity to have companionship. His hurt was so deep and his loneliness was more than he could stand. He saw this new friend as one who could help him forget the pain of his loss and move on. This was a mistake. He was overly dependent on his new friend. She could see that it was too soon for him to have a serious relationship. She liked this man but knew that he was using her as a solution to his grief. She broke off the relationship.

One is not ready to be a good spouse until he has done the difficult grief work that takes a minimum of a year. To be a good spouse, one must learn to be at peace with being single, or widowed. It is not fair to ask someone to do for you what he cannot possibly do. Another spouse cannot heal the pain of your grief. Another spouse can never take the place of your spouse who has died. Remember--put on the brakes and make no hasty decisions you might later regret.

THE BLESSING OF WORK, WITH RESERVATIONS

David was the greatest king of Israel, ever. He grieved over his dying son. He wept. He prayed. He fasted. But then seven days later his son died. He washed, changed his clothes, went into the house of the Lord and worshiped. He then went to his own house and he asked for food to eat. "Then his servants said to him, 'what is this thing that you have done? You fasted and wept for the child while it was alive; but when the child died, you rose and ate food.' He said, 'While the child was still alive, I fasted and wept; for I said, Who knows? The Lord may be gracious to me, and the child may live. But now he is dead; why should I fast? Can I bring him back again? I shall go to him, but he will not return to me'." (II Samuel 12:21-23.)

If you are not retired, you have to keep going to work after the funeral. Your energy is depleted and numbness permeates your spirit with grief. But you still go to work. Financial necessity dictates this for most people. However, it is important to see your work as a blessing. For a few hours each day, your mind and heart are rested from the full weight of the grief. When you return home or when you face the weekends, you must again face the full weight of your loss. See your work as a blessing. If you are retired, look for projects you can do around the house. To work and to pray-- these are the prescriptions for grief.

Some people are less verbal than others. They often deal with grief through work more than words. Ann Kaiser Stearns tells about an insurance salesman who was grieved to hear that his first child was a Down's Syndrome baby. Six days later he began tearing down the rickety wooden porch on the back of the couple's home. He had intended to rebuild the wooden porch anyway. Now he was tearing down the old one, piece by piece, using scarcely any tools for assistance. This young father was not resisting his grief. Although he was able to be of emotional comfort to his wife, he was never able to put his own feelings into words. One evening after another, he went out to the old porch he was violently

18

disassembling. Later on, he went out to the new porch he began to build. Eventually feelings of sorrow and anger were largely worked through. He began, unapologetically, to love their special needs child. His healing process was well underway. (*Living Through Personal Crisis*, p. 65)

This a good example of how grief is dealt with in different ways. All need to talk about it but some will work through it by using work or physical exercise. Karl Wallenda and his family were perhaps the greatest high-wire acrobats in the world. In 1962 several members of the Wallenda troupe fell from the wire and were killed while performing in Detroit, Michigan. Just a few days later it was announced that those who survived would be back on the high wire repeating their famous act. When a reporter questioned Karl Wallenda, the senior member of the troop, about the decision, he said, "To be on the wire is life. All else is waiting."(Cf. The Relational Revolution by Bruce Larson, p. 89)

There is a play called *Quilters*. It is the story of a couple moving west and living on the Great Plains. Life was hard. He was a railroad man. One day, working in the yard, the wife heard horses and looked up to see her husband's co-workers from the railroad. Her eyes fell on a basket they carried. They told her he'd been working on the tracks, there was a terrible accident, and he was killed. His friends took him to the family burial plot and buried him. The wife thanked them, and they rode away. She walked into the house she'd walked out of as a wife and now re-entered as a widow. She went directly to the back bedroom, sat down in a rocker, and did not move. The next day a relative who had heard the news came by to sit with her and found her rocking in the bedroom, apparently there since the previous day. She did not speak, but she lifted the woman's hands and put some quilting squares on her lap and a threaded needle in her hands. And in the midst of numbing pain, her hands began to recall what her mind could not.

Work can be a blessing in a time of grief. We must

grieve as we meet the everyday responsibilities of our life. We must keep going.

Keep a-Goin'

"If you strike a thorn or rose,
     Keep a-goin'!
If it hails or if it snows,
     Keep a-goin'!
'Taint no use to sit an'whine
When the fish ain't on your line;
Bait your hook an' keep a-tryin'-
     Keep a-goin'!
When the weather kills your crop,
     Keep a-goin'!
Though 'tis work to reach the top,
     Keep a-goin'!
S'pose you're out o' ev'ry dime,
Gittin' broke ain't any crime;
Tell the world you're feelin' *prime*--
     Keep a-goin'!
When it looks like all is up,
     Keep a-goin'!
Drain the sweetness from the cup,
     Keep a-goin'!
See the wild birds on the wing,
Hear the bells that sweetly ring,
When you feel like sighin', sing-
     Keep a-goin'!"

Frank L. Stanton p. 135
One Hundred and One Famous Poems

THE DEVIL IS ALWAYS CLOSE BY, WAITING

It is important to be aware of definite dangers that are inherent for all grieving. This is a vulnerable time. You are hurt. You are lonely. You are depressed. You mind does not function normally. Pain is your constant companion. It is crucial that you be alert to tragic mistakes that you can make.

I was told of a widow in our community who lost her husband. She began to deal with her pain by going to the riverboat casino. The time spent gambling made her forget the grief and pain of her situation. She ended up squandering the life savings for which she and her husband had worked hard and long. She even illegally went into trust funds that were earmarked for her children. She was obviously out of control. Guilt was then added to her grief.

Gambling, alcoholism, overspending, over-eating-- these and other kinds of addictions are possible temptations for those in grief. I Peter 5:8,9 warns us: "Be self-controlled and alert. Your enemy the devil prowls around like a roaring lion looking for someone to devour.. Resist him, standing firm in the faith."

You must be aware of false "highs" that would take you briefly from your grief. The addictions that enslave human beings give a form of "high" feeling. On the surface, it looks like this is the answer to a better life. But the "high" proves to be temporary and the desire for this feeling returns again and again. One becomes enslaved to these false highs and it is very difficult to become free of them. You must be on your toes.

There are other ways the devil works. Addictions are only a small part of his arsenal. Dorothee Soelle in her book, *Suffering* suggests that "the most important question we can ask about suffering is whom it serves. Does our suffering serve God or the devil, the cause of becoming alive or being morally paralyzed?" The question we must ask is not "where does the tragedy come from?" but "Where does it lead?" This is the main issue. Soelle asks us if we are going to be martyrs for God or martyrs for the devil? If our grief leaves us doubting God and doubting the world's goodness or doubting our own purpose for existence, then we become "the devil's martyrs". (Cf. Harold S. Kushner, *When Bad Things Happen To Good People*, Schocken Books: New York, 1981, p. 138)

The main issue, according to Soelle is not the circumstances surrounding our grief but our reaction to it. Will we let our grief destroy us, or will we let our grief lead us to new faith, strength and love? We must make the choice for life, for God, and for ourselves. This is essential. This is what determines our future healing.

A TREE SPEAKS--YOU ARE NEEDED

One day I was home by myself, and that particular day I was having a pity party of mine own. I was comparing myself unfavorably to everyone in the world. Looking out the back window I saw a tree that I had seen a million times- a mulberry tree. Only this time was different. I saw that tree and it dawned on me that this tree had a space all its own. This tree was taking up perhaps a square foot in my back yard. It was saying to me..."This is my space. This is where I belong." It had a memorable effect on me and my state of mind. If this tree has a space and this tree belongs, then there is a place for me in this world. I belong wherever God plants me. No, I am not a tree, but I am a human being and human beings are more precious than trees.

So, when I am in a state of self doubt, I remember that mulberry tree. I belong. I belong here. I have my space that is sacred. I can make my contribution that is unique. These are thoughts that I need to keep in mind at all times, especially when I am down on myself.

In *The Dilemma of Love*, Susan Cooley Ricketson gives us twelve things we need to say to ourselves each day and night. They are truth-filled affirmations that help us keep the right perspective when we are depressed and despondent.

1. I am a precious human being who cannot be replaced on this planet.

2. There is only one me and I am responsible to nurture my gifts and to let my light shine.

3. I am in charge of my life and the path I choose.

4. My first priority is my own well-being and the journey of my soul.

5. I am responsible for my attitudes, feelings and behavior. I do not assume responsibility for those of others.

6. As my behavior becomes more appropriate, my success grows.

7. I am a fallible human being who makes mistakes. I learn from my mistakes and am accountable for them.

8. I am not inferior or superior to anyone else.

9. I deserve to be treated with dignity.

10. I am gentle and loving to myself.

11. I am patient with myself.

12. There is plenty of time. I have the rest of my life to continue to grow. (p. 191)

Remind yourself often that you are now in a state of grief depression. Your thoughts and perspectives may often be in need of correction. Keep a close watch over the way you talk to yourself.

Zig Zigler in his book *See You At The Top* gives fifteen steps to building a healthy self image. If ever our self image takes at beating, it is when we lose someone precious to us. Here are his suggestions:

"1. Take inventory with the full realization that no one on the face of this earth can make you feel inferior without your permission. Only you can make that important decision to build up a sense of self worth.

23

2. Make up, dress up, go up--improve your personal appearance.

3. Regularly read Horatio Alger stories of people who overcome all kinds of obstacles and handicaps.

4. Listen to the speakers, teachers and ministers who build up mankind

5. Build a healthy self image with a series of short steps.

6. Join the smile and compliment club. The most destitute person in the world is the one without a smile.

7. Do something for someone else. No one is useless in this world who lightens the burden of it to anyone else.

8. Be careful of your associates. Deliberately associate with people of a high moral character who look on the bright side of life and the benefits will be enormous. You acquire much of the thinking, mannerisms and characteristics of the people you are around.

9. Make a list of your positive qualities on a card and keep it for handy reference.

10 Make a victory list to remind you of your past successes. This should extend from your childhood to the present time.

11. There are some things you must avoid--pornography--they degrade your fellow man and yourself.

12. Learn from the successful failures. Babe Ruth struck out more times than any man in baseball history.

13. Join an organization with worthwhile goals that requires you to participate by speaking.

14. Look yourself and them in the eye.

15. Alter your physical appearance when possible, practical and desirable."

In the final analysis, we must work hard at focusing on our faith for it is there that we get the correct self-image and it is there that we are placed in the midst of people who have a "good news" outlook toward self, others and the future.

IS IT A SIN TO CRY?

Early in my ministry, an elderly physician died. I met with the family and we prepared for the funeral. His widow took me aside and asked me: "Is it a sin to cry?" Her sons had told her to be strong and to be dignified in this time of sadness.

Here is an example of how family and friends can give you the wrong advice in facing grief. You must be wise and discerning what advice to accept and what advice to reject. I answered her question by quoting the shortest verse in the Bible. John 11:35 says: "Jesus wept." It was at the funeral of his friend Lazarus that Jesus wept. Openly he showed his emotions. This is very important.

Jesus said in the Sermon on the Mount, "Blessed are those who mourn for they will be comforted." (Matthew 5:4)The opposite is also true, "Cursed are those that try to avoid mourning for they will not find comfort!"

God has not made you like the trees and the mountains and the stars and the planets. He made you in His own image. You are a human being. You must allow your feelings to surface. You will have the whole gamut of emotions. Your emotions will be on the surface for awhile. It is important that you express your emotions rather than deny them.

Dr. Joyce Brothers lost her husband Milt to cancer and some time later wrote a helpful book entitled *Widowed*. In this book she makes the following observation about tears. "Sigmund Freud wrote rather paradoxically, that

25

remembering was the best way to forget. It is as if each time you remember, a healing film grows over the memory until eventually it is no longer a raw wound. You are whole and healthy again. There may be a scar, but you are ready to forge ahead in life. The memories and the tears they provoke are partners in the healing process. Tears are not only physically helpful, making the widow feel better; they are psychologically helpful as well. The more a widow cries and eases the pain of her loss with tears, the more she becomes conditioned to her loss. Becoming conditioned to it reduces its pain. There comes a time when she can think of her husband without pain, without tears." p. 93.

I have two theories about tears. I believe that women outlive men by about seven years and the reason is they express their emotions more readily. Men are more prone to hold their emotions in check. My second theory is that every time you cry or have tears come to your eyes, you are a step closer to healing. Your tears are a way of bringing your pain out into the light of day where your emotional pain can be healed. Do not be afraid of your tears. Your tears are your built in way of letting off pressure from the inner pain of your heart. Those that mourn are those that find comfort.

DON'T WORSHIP OR ENSHRINE

One of the issues that the grieving person has to deal with is the personal belongings of the deceased. What should one do? This is not a question that can be answered simply. There are some things which with you might never part. There are a few things that might be parted with immediately. Most things will be parted with over time.

It would be extreme to give away everything that reminds one of his loved one. But there is another extreme-- keeping and hallowing all the personal belongings of the deceased. I once visited in the home of an older couple who showed me their son's room. Their son had been killed in Europe during World War II and buried there. His room was just as he left it the day he went off to war. A couple of ties were draped over a chair. His clothes were hanging in the closet. He had a new car when he left for the war. It was out in the barn, unmoved and untouched, covered with dust.. This was twenty years after his death.

This was a futile effort on his mother's part to keep him alive, to keep his memory alive. She could not bear to touch or move her son's belongings. His room had become a shrine. In a way, this is a form of idolatry. It is a reluctance to let go and surrender the departed to God. We must worship the One that will never leave us or forsake us. We must not elevate anyone to the point of worship. Yes, it is painful to let go. But in letting go, we do not diminish the memory or the importance of those departed. In letting go, we trust God to take better care of our loved one than we ever could. In letting go, we recognize and proclaim that this world is not our eternal abiding place and that God has a home prepared for us that is far superior to the one we have here on this earth.

SORCERY—A PAGAN PRACTICE

Grief makes us want to see our loved ones and to talk to them. Sorcery is the attempt to communicate with the dead. Ancient peoples made this a part of their religion. It is a subject that is dealt with in the Scripture. It was seen as a demonic practice. God's people were warned to avoid such endeavors.

Deuteronomy 18:10-12 says "Let no one be found among you who sacrifices his son or daughter in the fire, who practices divination or sorcery, interprets omens, engages in witchcraft, or casts spells, or who is a medium or spiritist or who consults the dead. Anyone who does these things is detestable to the Lord."

II Kings 17:17 says "They practiced divination and sorcery and sold themselves to do evil in the eyes of the Lord, provoking him to anger."

Malachi 3:5 says, "So I will come near to you for

judgment. I will be quick to testify against sorcerers, adulterers and perjurers..." says the Lord Almighty.

The New Testament equally speaks out against sorcery as an evil of that day. Paul was opposed by a sorcerer by the name of Elymas. Acts 13:9-10 reads: Then Saul, who was also called Paul, filled with the Holy Spirit, looked straight at Elymas and said, "You are a child of the devil and an enemy of everything that is right! You are full of all kinds of deceit and trickery. Will you never stop perverting the right ways of the Lord?"

Sorcery is mentioned four times in the book of Revelation: 9:21; 18:23; 21:8; 22:15. It is always seen as a sin against God. It is not God's will for us to communicate with the dead. He wants us to communicate with Him!

However, this is not a sin that has been left by the wayside as an ancient practice. It has always been with us. As people have less and less faith in God, the more they will turn to pagan practices such as fortune tellers, witchcraft, psychics, astrologers and communicating with the dead.

As these words are being written there is a growing popularity with sorcery. Just about everyday of the week one can turn on the television to one or more programs where a medium will help people get in touch with loved ones who have gone on. It is no longer called "sorcery". The more sophisticated title of "crossing over" is being used.

In your grief, you may be tempted to try this out. Resist this temptation. It will not be the answer you are looking for. Your answer is found in turning to the living God not some spiritual advisor who is anxious to take your money. Communicating with God is the answer to your grief.

TWO LESSONS FROM JOB

Here are two lessons from Job, the main grief book of the Bible.

1. Remember you are not God. Life is a gift, loaned

2. God is better at running the universe and you are better at learning from Him.

In his book, *Notes to Myself*, Hugh Prather tells of sitting by the bedside of his wife as she was sleeping while very ill. He wrote:

"She may die before morning. But I have been with her for four years. Four years. There is no way I could feel cheated if I didn't have her for another day. I didn't deserve her for one minute, God knows.

And I may die before morning.

What I must do is die now. I must accept the justice of death and the injustice of life. I have lived a good life-- longer than many, better than most. Tony died when he was twenty. I have had thirty-two years. I couldn't ask for another day. What did I do to deserve birth? It was a gift. I am me-that is a miracle. I had no right to a single minute. Some are given a single hour. And yet I have had thirty-two years.

Few can choose when they will die. I choose to accept death now. As of this moment I give up my "right" to live. And I give up my "right" to her life. But it's morning. I have been given another day. Another day to hear and read and smell and walk and love and glory. I am alive for another day." (1970 Real People Press)

If we are not careful, we give into the belief that God could do better in the past than He can do in the present or future. This is limiting God. Our nostalgia can be a grand form of unbelief and minimizing the power of God. Ecclesiastes 7:10 offers these words of wisdom: "Do not say, 'Why were the old days better than these?' For it is not wise to ask such questions." God is the Eternal Now. We must move from a "past tense" view of God. He gives you a positive future...a hope for today and tomorrow. It would be wise to ask: "What new thing is God about to work in my life? What new truth is He about to teach me? What joy is awaiting me just around the corner?" William Temple said "This world can be saved from political chaos and collapse by one thing only and that is worship!" And of course he was talking about the worship of God. We must trust God to give us this day the glory that is not just past tense. With God's help, we can find the glory of today, every day.

The Second lesson that Job would give us is the question: Could we do a better job at running the universe than God does? We are so prone to call God into question. How would we run things if we were in charge? Would we eliminate all suffering? If we did, we would eliminate all the good that comes from suffering. The greatest music, the greatest art, and the greatest literature have in it the background of sorrow and tragedy and grief. If we had no sorrow or grief, would we really be better people? Or, would we even be more arrogant and selfish? Heavy questions make us know that we have no business even thinking about running the universe! We are much better by letting God run the universe and trust Him to bring good even out of the wrong choices people make. Romans 8:28 says: "In all things God works to bring about good to those that love Him and are called according to His purpose." Think real hard. What bad thing has happened to you in the past, but God turned it into good? That is something to think about right now. God is working to bring good to you in your grief.

ONE DAY AT A TIME

The wisdom of Jesus will never be matched. He was the author and finisher of our faith. He is the epitome of all wisdom and truth. His teachings will never be outdated. His truth endures through all generations. He was a master at short, pithy sayings that are easily remembered. In the

Sermon on the Mount, Jesus chided his followers not to worry. He called on us to have faith in the Father that provides our needs. He said, "Therefore do not worry about tomorrow, for tomorrow will worry about itself. Each day has enough trouble of its own." Matthew 6:34.

Sir William Osler gave a speech to the students at Yale University. He called it "A Way of Life". This is what he said:

"I have a message that may be helpful. It is not philosophical, nor is it strictly moral or religious...and yet in a way it is all three. It is so simple that some of you may turn away disappointed. My message is but a word, a Way.

"The way of life that I preach is a habit to be acquired gradually by long and steady repetition. It is the practice of living for the day only, and for the day's work, living in "day-tight compartments." The chief worries of life arise from the foolish habit of looking before and after.

"A few months ago I stood on the bridge of a great liner, plowing the ocean at twenty-five knots. "She is alive in every plate," said the Captain, "a huge monster with brain and nerves, an immense stomach, a wonderful heart and lungs, and a splendid system of locomotion." Just at that moment a signal sounded, and all over the ship the watertight compartments were closed. "Our chief factor of safety," said the Captain.

"Now each of you is a much more marvelous organization than the great liner and bound on a longer voyage. What I urge is that you so learn to control the machinery as to live with "day-tight compartments" as the most certain way to insure safety on the voyage. Get on the bridge, and see that at least the great bulkheads are in working order. Touch a button and hear, at every level of your life, the iron doors shutting out the Past--the dead yesterdays. Touch another and shut off, with a metal curtain, the Future--the unborn tomorrows. Then you are safe, safe for today.

"The load of tomorrow, added to that of yesterday, carried today makes the strongest falter. Waste of energy, mental distress, and nervous worries dog the steps of a man who is anxious about the future. Shut close, then, the great fore and aft bulkheads, and prepare to cultivate the habit of life in "day-tight compartments!

"I am simply giving you a philosophy of life that I have found helpful in my work. In this philosophy or way of life each of you may learn to drive the straight furrow, and so come to the true measure of a man." (*Light from Many Lamps*, Lillian Eichler Watson, pp. 233-4)

YOU ARE NOT AN EAGLE RIGHT NOW!

Isaiah 40 describes God as never growing weak or weary. He is the source of strength for those that are weak and weary but they put their hope in the Lord. Then he describes three times in a persons life experience. First, there are those that "soar on wings like eagles." These are the times when we are doing so great. We are on the mountain top. We feel the ecstasy of life and strength. It is not too often that we are in this kind of state of being.

The second period that Isaiah describes is when we are "running but not growing weary." This would be the more ordinary times of our life. We are keeping a busy schedule, meeting our responsibilities and running.

But then Isaiah describes another kind of time in our life when we "will walk and not be faint." In other words, there are times when all we can do is put one foot in the front of the other and not faint.

Now that describes you. You are not soaring with the eagles. You are not running. You are barely moving...walking one step at a time. That is you! Everybody ends up in grief or crisis sooner or later. So, don't even try to run or to fly through the days. Just keep your feet on the ground and make it through the day with faith. Then, as you trust on the Lord, you will find a silent strength coming into your life. Little by little, the pain will begin to lift and you will be able to run and not grow weary. But that is not today.

DOUBT CAN LEAD TO FAITH

Grief recovery is a time when our faith takes a beating. We all are a mixture of faith and doubt. Some have more faith and some have more doubt. We have a choice as to whether we will feed our faith or feed our doubt.

First let's say a word about doubt. Doubt asks questions and that is the positive side of doubt. If we do not ask questions, we certainly do not get answers! Shakespeare put it this way:

"Modest doubt is call'd

The beacon of the wise, the tent that searches

To the bottom of the worst."

(II, ii, 15Troilus and Cressida)

It is in times of doubt and trouble that we need faith the most. Anyone can believe when things are going great. When your world is tumbling it is the time when you need faith to continue. Here we find the value of faith. Faith is so important as it speaks of our view of the future. Faith says there is a future. Doubt says there is none. Faith says that God will see you through this crisis. Doubt says life will never get better. It is very critical that we not chastise ourselves for questions during a time of crisis and at the same time it is critical that we look for ways to feed our faith when our faith is very weak.

Remember the man that came to Jesus and said, "I do believe; help me overcome my unbelief."(Mark 9:24) This needs to be our prayer during this time of crisis. Faith is like the plants in your house. They need to be watered. They need some sunshine to grow. So it is with our faith. Someone found scribbled on the wall of a basement in Germany at the close of World War II these words: "I believe in the sun, even when it is not shining. I believe in love, even when I cannot feel it. I believe in God, even when He is silent." We must reach down into the deepest recesses of our hearts and find that God is there! We are not alone. We can make it through this valley.

What can a person do when he finds his prayers bouncing back from the ceiling? George Macdonald has this advice:

"Fold the arms of your faith and wait in quietness until the light goes up in your darkness. Fold the arms of your faith, I say, but not of your action. Think of something you ought to do, and go do it. Heed not your feelings. Do your work."

(*A Feast For a Time of Fasting*, Louis Cassels, p.51)

THE WILL OF GOD

In the days of our grief we will hear people say, "This is the will of God. We must accept it." These words can come across to us as very harsh and cause us to have anger toward God. We can begin to accuse God of taking our loved one from us. We need to take a long hard look at "the will of God". What is meant by that phrase?

Much of our thinking is colored by the oversimplified belief that everything that happens is the will of God. Is that true? Or can we see things that happen with which God had nothing to do with or were in direct contradiction to the will of God? Is there evil in our world and does evil sometimes win out? We know that Hitler gassed 6 million Jewish people during World War II. Was that the will of God? I think not. It is very important that we not accuse God of masterminding all the evil that takes place in our world.

I like the humorous story of the little boy who was telling his friend how he drowned a cat. "I dumped him under the water and held him a long time. When I brought him up he was spurting and spewing. Then I dumped him again and held him there." At this point the boy realized his pastor had walked up and was listening to this sordid conversation. So he added, "And the Lord took him." We sometimes put blame on God that in no way fits.

Steffanie Powers suffered the loss of two of her closest friends within hours. William Holden, intoxicated, fell in his apartment, cut his head, and bled to death. Natalie Wood, intoxicated, slipped from her boat and drowned. Ms Powers asked a reporter what many misguided and unthinking people have asked. "How can a loving God do a thing like this?" Again, we must ask the question: Is everything that happens the will of God?

So, what is the will of God? Leslie Weatherhead was a Methodist minister in London, England during World War II and he wrestled with this subject and wrote a little booklet called *The Will of God*. In this booklet he tried to show that God's will must be understood in three different ways. First there is God's intentional will. Then there is God's circumstantial will. And finally there is God's ultimate will.

First, *God's intentional will* is for us is similar to the goals that any parents would have for their children. God wants us to be protected from evil, danger and pain. If God's perfect will was realized there would be no sin and no evil and no suffering in this world. This world would be like heaven. There would be no diseases like cancer, no murder and no natural calamities.

But God's intentional will is often frustrated. In other words, God doesn't always get His way! Murders do happen. Suffering takes place. People rebel against His plan. That brings us to the second dimension of God's Will. *God's circumstantial will*. When bad things happen, God then has a plan and a purpose to intervene and make the best of the imperfect circumstances. All hope is not lost when evil occurs or sickness comes or war breaks out. God still is actively involved in His world. He works to give people strength and courage and faith to deal with the crisis at hand and to make the best of the worst circumstances. God is available in the valley if we will turn to Him.

Then there is God's ultimate will. God is able to take the worst and bring about His best. He is able to work things out for good. He even can use evil and turn it into a great good. Weatherhead uses the cross of Jesus Christ as a perfect example of God's will. God's perfect will was for people to recognize who Jesus was and to love and worship him. But this did not happen. They crucified him on the cross, so God worked with the circumstances that were there. God brought about his Ultimate Will by transforming the cross from the greatest evil to the greatest good. "And we know that in all things God works for good of those who love him, who have been called according to his purpose." (Romans 8:28) Today the cross is the most famous symbol in the world. It is the inspiration of millions of people. It represents the power and love of God.

There is a story about a Chinese farmer who had a horse and a son. One day, his horse broke out of the corral and fled to the freedom of the hills. "Your horse got out? What bad luck!" said his neighbors. "Why?" the old Chinese asked. "How do you know it's bad luck?"

The next night the horse came back to the corral leading twelve wild stallions. The farmer's son saw the thirteen horses in the corral, slipped out, and locked the gate. Now, the farmer had thirteen horses instead of one. The neighbors heard the news and came to the farmer, "Oh, you have thirteen horses! What good luck!" The old Chinese answered, "How do you know that is good luck?"

Later, the strong young son was trying to break one of the stallions only to be thrown off, breaking a leg. The neighbors came back: "You son broke his leg? What bad luck!" Again, the wise father commented, "How do you know it's bad luck?"

A few days later a Chinese warlord came through the territory and conscripted every able-bodied young man, taking them off to war, never to return again. The young son was passed over because of his broken leg.

36

When bad things happen to us, we must reserve our final judgment of things. In the end, the bad can be overshadowed by the good. (cf Rev. John William Zehring in article "When Bad Things Happen To You" in *Marriage and Family Living*, April 1987, p. 20)

God's will is always for our ultimate good. We may not see any of it right now. That is why we might rebel when people say our grief is the will of God. God does not want us to suffer grief. But in our grief, he has a high and noble plan that will ultimately bring out the best in us.

MEMORIES-A MOVEABLE FEAST

Ernest Hemingway wrote an autobiography retracing his early days as a writer in Paris. The book was written after his death and is entitled *A Moveable Feast* (Scribner, 1964). In a letter to a friend, Hemingway wrote, "If you are lucky enough to have lived in Paris as a young man, then wherever you go for the rest of your life, it stays with you, for Paris is a moveable feast."

Let me suggest that good and happy memories that you have of your departed loved one can be a moveable feast. Wherever you are, you can bring to memory the good times that you enjoyed together. Think of your happiest occasions. Relive them. Feast on them. Do not look on these memories as being painful. See just the opposite. See these memories as joyful moments invested in your life. Our memory is like a bank. We invest money in a bank. We invest memories into our heart. Those good memories inspire us and lift us up. You might want to try writing down some of the most outstanding times you shared with your loved one. Keep those memories strong.

Sometimes we lose someone after months of illness and suffering. Sometimes their appearance changes. Sometimes their minds become clouded and confused. It is important that we not remember them in this way, but remember them in earlier days when they were truly themselves. You are richer because of the good memories that live within your heart. An old hymn written by J.B.F. Wright is entitled: *Precious Memories*.

"Precious memories, unseen angels,

sent from somewhere to my soul;

How they linger, ever near me,

and the sacred past unfold.

Precious father, loving mother,

fly across the lonely years;

And old home scenes of my childhood,

in fond memory appears.

In the stillness of the midnight,

echoes from the past I hear;

Old-time singing, gladness bringing,

from that lovely land some-where.

As I travel on t life's pathway,

know not what the years may hold;

As I ponder hope grows fonder,

precious memories flood my soul."

PAINFUL MEMORIES

If your loved one did not die suddenly, it just may be that there was some suffering and pain in his life. My dad suffered for ten years before he died. He had arthritis. He also suffered from three unsuccessful back surgeries. He progressively grew more incapacitated. He eventually could not raise his arms. He eventually went to a walker and then to a wheelchair. He then lost his eyesight. He then became bedfast. Pain was his constant companion during this time.

When I think of bringing my dad back to this earth, I know I would never want to do that. In fact, I started praying for God to take him Home some months before he died. It is so hard to watch a loved one suffer. Painful memories are a part of my grief recovery.

I can remember the day I went to the cleaners. I had a suit, a shirt and a tie to be cleaned. They belonged to my dad. My dad would be wearing these in his casket. To this day, that stands out as a very painful experience. It just had to be done. I did it for my dad. It helps to see that we were there for our loved ones in their time of need.

THE HEAVENLY GRANDSTANDS

In earlier days, there was a greater emphasis on heaven. We have not made this world a better place by misplacing that emphasis. In this time of your grief, heaven will become more real and that is the way it should be. The Bible talks about how we are surrounded by such a great cloud of witnesses." (Hebrews 12:1) This is talking about those that have gone on before us. They are looking down from heaven encouraging us and inspiring us to run the race of faith and courage.

Vachel Lindsay has a poem entitled "General William Booth Enters Into Heaven," which is in poetic fashion imagines the entry into heaven by the great founder of the Salvation Army. The last stanza reads:

"And when Booth halted by the curb for prayer

He saw his Master through the flag-filled air.

Christ came gently with a robe and crown

For Booth the soldier, while the throng knelt down.

He saw King Jesus. They were face to face,

And he knelt a-weeping in that holy place.

Are you washed in the blood of the Lamb?"

I was walking through the intensive care unit of one of our hospitals one day when I heard someone call my name. I turned to go into one of those little cubicles where I found Mr. Lee Buchanan, an old friend. He was hooked up to tubes running every which way. He wanted to talk to me. He said to me, "You may have trouble believing this, but I died the other day." I asked for him to tell me more. He went on to tell me that a day or two prior to this his heart had stopped. He described the scene that took place. The doctors came rushing and he felt his soul leaving his body. He said he tried to raise up to catch it. Then it was like he was looking down from above watching the medical staff work on him. His soul came back into his body and he survived.

Our natural tendency is to question such a story but as he was telling it he had tears running down his face. He said to me, "I will never fear death again. It was the most wonderful feeling I have ever had. I will never be afraid to die again. Some people don't believe what I am saying but it is true." It was hard not to believe what he was saying. He had no reason to lie with such emotions. As I left that room I knew that this is the way God wants us to feel about death. He wants us to be prepared for death. He wants us to meet death with faith and trust.

Norman Vincent Peale has the following story to tell.

"When recently the wife of a friend died, he was, of course, devastated. But I was impressed by the depth and quality of his mental victory over his great loss and sorrow. He told me that shortly after his wife's passing he 'felt' her presence most definitely and 'by an inner ear' heard her speak to him. He thanked her for coming to comfort him and plaintively said, 'Please come to me soon again.' To which she answered, 'Why, I am always near to you.' Asked how he felt about the reality of this experience, he answered simply, 'I'm excited to realize that she lives. She is not dead but alive. Isn't that wonderful?'" (*The Positive Principle*, p. 238.)

If we can see that our loved one is not dead, but alive, it will be a great comfort to us. Heaven will be more precious to us. God wants us to have that heavenly vision that Thomas Edison had. On his death bed, the great inventor gave his last words on this earth, "It's beautiful over there." One of the reasons why it is beautiful over there is our loved ones are there. They are with us and at the same time, they are in heaven! That is a paradox. For those of us that are Christians, we can understand that for that is the way Jesus Christ is to us. He is with us, yet he is in heaven.

Joyce Brothers was left behind when her husband Milt died. She tells of something that helped her. "My great weapon against loneliness, however, was something Milt once told me. I cannot understand how I could have forgotten it but I had until a year after Milt died when I woke up remembering how he had comforted me when my father died. 'He has not left you," Milt had said. 'I believe that, even in death, people remain a part of their family. I believe that children carry with them a part of their parents' souls and consciousness. I believe that husbands and wives remain part of each other.'

"I lay there in the bed thinking about what he had said and I knew he was right. Milt was part of me, and if he was part of me, how could I be lonely? I cannot tell you how much this memory helped. I am not saying that I went from loneliness to happiness in a day, but from that time on everything began to get a little better." (*Widowed*, pp. 134f)

We must keep in mind that we are not alone. We are surrounded by the great cloud of witnesses of those that have gone on before us. They influence us and inspire us. They will not come to us but we will go to them.

ISOLATION OR MINISTRY?

One of the best things we can do when we suffer loss is to ask the question: Why am I here? What is the purpose of my life? What is there to live for? As we find the answer to those questions we find motivation to keep going.

Viktor Frankl was imprisoned for three years at Auschwitz and other Nazi concentration camps. He miraculously survived that Holocaust experience only to find

41

out that his entire family had been killed. Out of this suffering and meaninglessness, he wrote the classic book *Man's Search for Meaning.* Here is one of his conclusions: "There is nothing in the world, I venture to say, that would so effectively help one to survive even the worst conditions, as the knowledge that there is meaning in one's life. There is much wisdom in the words of Nietzsche: 'He who has a *why* to live for can bear almost any *how.*' What people actually need is not a tensionless state but rather the striving and struggling for some goal worthy of themselves." (pp.164,166)

What is the purpose of your life? What are you here for? Perhaps the answer to that question is found in the answer to the question: "**Who is it that needs me?**" When you can answer that question and not dodge it, you will begin to find motivation to move forward in your life.

Jeannette Kupferman describes the progress of her grief journey in her autobiographical book *When the Crying's Done: A Journey Through Widowhood.* She says: "Another neighbor has died on the Terrace leaving a widow in her fifties--an extremely pleasant cheerful woman who volunteered her help again and again when Jacqust, my husband was in the hospital. I seem to be called upon to comfort mourners more and more often. In the beginning I found it difficult. I had little comfort to give. Now I almost feel that I have grown into a role of professional mourner and comforter--that indeed I have a special qualification for the role. I feel part of a band of women--a group of 'wise women' if you wish--whose baptism and initiation through fire has given them a special role to play as collaborator, sympathizer with them in their suffering. It does not depress me. On the contrary, it gives my life new meaning. I have entered the ranks of the wise."(p. 95)

In the first weeks and even months of your grief, you may have little energy or motivation to comfort anyone. You will be in such grief that you will need to be mourning in a selfish way. This is necessary. This is not wrong. But as time

42

passes, you will find people who are hurting just as bad as you and you can reach out to them. You are called to be a minister to others. You have special qualifications. You can empathize as many others cannot. It is time to reach out. You have a mission. You have a purpose. Your life has a meaning. As you comfort others, the comfort of God will come back to comfort you!

There is an old Chinese tale about a woman whose only son died. In her grief, she went to the holy man and said, "what prayers, what magical incantations do you have to bring my son back to life?"

Instead of sending her away or reasoning with her, he said to her, "Fetch me a mustard seed from a home that has never known sorrow. We will use it to drive the sorrow out of your life."

The woman set off at once in search of that magical mustard seed. She came first to a splendid mansion, knocked at the door, and said, "I am looking for a home that has never known sorrow. Is this such a place? It is very important to me." They told her, "You've certainly come to the wrong place," and began to describe all the tragic things that had recently befallen them. The woman said to herself, "Who is better able to help these poor, unfortunate people than I who have had misfortune of my own?"

She stayed to comfort them, then went on in he search for a home that had never had or known sorrow. But wherever she turned, in hovels and in palaces, she found one tale after another of sadness and misfortune. Ultimately, she became so involved in ministering to other people's grief that she forgot about her quest for the magical mustard seed, never realizing that it had in fact driven the sorrow out of her life. (Cf. *When Bad Things Happen to Good People*, Harold S. Kushner, pp. 110f.)

Here is one answer to our grief recovery. When we reach out to others who are suffering, we find ourselves being touched by the healing love of God. If we will only open our eyes and ears and ask God to show us those that we can help, we will find opportunities to minister and to care.

B.H. Carroll became the founder and President of Southwestern Baptist Theological Seminary in Ft. Worth, Texas. On the day he was converted to Christ, he returned home from church and wrote in his diary:

"Write thy name on my head

   that I may think for thee.

Write thy name on my lips

   that I may speak for thee;

Write thy name on my feet

   that I may walk with and for thee;

Write thy name on my hands

   that I may work with and for thee;

Write thy name on my ears

   that I may listen for thee;

Write thy name on my heart

   that I may love thee;

Write thy name on my shoulders

   that I may bear burdens for thee;

Write thy name on my eyes

   that I may see for thee;

Write thy name all over me

   that I may be wholly thine—

   always and everywhere."

(cf. *Has God Called You?* by Henlee Barnette, p. 109f.)

God has a plan, a very special plan just for you. Ask Him and He will show you what that is.

DEATH BE NOT PROUD: MINIMIZING THE FEAR

My three year old grandson, Beau, came to the

kitchen table one Sunday as we were finishing our lunch and ask me to go to the bedroom to get my flashlight. I have one of those flashlights you plug into an electric socket and the battery recharges itself. Beau loves to play with this flashlight and usually he makes a bee-line to our bedroom to get that flashlight. But this day it was different.

I answered Beau, "You go get that flashlight. You know where it is." He said, "No, I can't. There's a monster in there." I said, "There is no monster in my bedroom. You know there is no monster in my bedroom." He would not take "no" for an answer. He kept insisting that I go with him to get that flashlight.

Finally I agreed and we walked hand in hand into the scary bedroom and I said, "See, there is no monster in here." He agreed and got the flashlight and went on about his business.

As I reflected over that conversation, I thought that this is the way we think about Death.

Death is a monster. Death is scary. Death is frightening…so frightening that we refuse to even talk about it or plan for it. But…that is all in our minds. When we go to Jesus with our fear of death, he walks with us and shows us that there is no monster. The monster is just a figment of our imagination. There is nothing to fear. Death is our passage-way to a more glorious future.

William Cullen Bryant penned these words when he was seventeen years old. The poem is called "Thanatopsis".

"So live, that when thy summons comes to join

The innumerable caravan, which moves

To that mysterious realm, where each shall take

His chamber in the silent halls of death,

Thou go not, like the quarry-slave at night,

Scourged to his dungeon, but, sustained and soothed

By an unfaltering trust, approach thy grave

Like one who wraps the drapery of his couch

About him, and lies down to pleasant dreams."

Tony Compolo tells of a funeral he attended at his home church--Mt. Carmel Baptist Church in West Philadelphia. Clarence, a college friend of his had been killed in a subway-train accident. At the beginning of the service, the pastor brilliantly expounded upon what the Bible says about the promise of the resurrection and the joys of being with Christ. Then he came down from the platform and went over to the right side of the sanctuary, where the family of Tony's dead friend was seated in the first three rows. There, he spoke special words of comfort for them.

Then the pastor did a most unusual thing. He went over to the open casket and spoke as though to the corpse. He said, "Clarence! Clarence! There were lot of things we should have said to you when you were alive which we never got around to saying to you. And I want to say them now."

What followed was a beautiful litany of memories of things that Clarence had done for many people present and for the church. The list recalled how lovingly Clarence served others without thought of reward. When he had finished, the pastor looked at Clarence's body and said, "Well, Clarence. Good Night!" And with that he slammed down the lid of the casket as a stunned silence fell over the congregation.

Then a beautiful smile slowly lit up the pastor's face and he shouted, "And I know that God is going to give Clarence a good morning!"

With that the choir rose to its feet and started singing, "On that great gettin' up morning we shall rise, we shall rise!" Then everyone in the congregation stood and starting singing, "On that great gettin' up morning we shall rise, we shall rise!" There was clapping and crying but the crying were tears of joy.

Celebration had broken out in the face of death. This should be our goal. God wants to take the sting out of death

46

for you. He wants to replace any fear that we have with a joyous faith. Paul deals with this subject in the fifteenth chapter of I Corinthians. He asks "Where, O death, is your victory? Where, O death, is your sting?"(I Corinthians 15:55)

Dr. Claude A. Frazier, a noted allergist, told a story in *The Upper Room* some years ago. The characters in this story were a boy and his father and the boy was one of those people who have violent reactions to bee stings. He had gone into convulsions previously. The next sting could kill him.

Driving down the road, a bee flew into the window of their car. When he saw the bee, the boy became hysterical. His father spoke reassuring words, pulled over to the side of the road, and caught the bee in his hand. A moment later he released it, and they boy became frantic again. The father, turning his palm toward the lad, said, "Son, you don't need to be afraid. See the barb of the stinger is imbedded here in the palm. I have taken the sting out of that insect and it can't harm you."

That is a parable of what Jesus Christ came to this earth to do. He took the sting out of death. The fear of that can send us into convulsions is taken away. We can face the future with hope. We can celebrate the lives of our loved ones that have passed on to the other side.

John Donne, the English poet mocked Death in his famous poem "Death Be Not Proud":

"Death, be not proud, though some have called thee

Mighty and dreadful, for thou are not so:

For those whom thou think'st thou dost overthrow

Die not, poor Death, nor yet canst thou kill me.

From rest and sleep, which but thy pictures be,

Much pleasure, then from thee much more must flow;

And soonest our best men with thee do go--

Rest of their bones and souls' delivery!

Thou'rt slave to fate, chance, kings, and desperate men,

And dost with poison, war, and sickness dwell;

And poppy or charms can make us sleep as well,

And better than thy stroke. Why swell'st thou then?

One short sleep past, we wake eternally,

And Death shall be no more: Death, thou shalt die."

(Cf. *Light From Many Lamps*, p. 116)

Fear maximizes grief and loss. Faith heals. Our faith speaks of eternal life. An anonymous author penned these words:

"I am standing upon the seashore. A ship at my side spreads her white sails to the morning breeze and starts for the blue ocean. She is an object of beauty and strength and I stand and watch her until at length she hangs like a speck of white cloud just where the sea and the sky come down to mingle with each other.

"Then someone at my side says, 'There! She's gone.' Gone where? Gone from my sight--that is all. She's just as large in mast and hull and spar as she was when she left my side and just as able to bear her load of living freight to the place of destination. Her diminished size is in me, not in her; and just at the moment when someone at my side says, 'There! She's gone,' there are other eyes watching her coming and other voices ready to take up the glad shout, 'There she comes'!"

"To be absent from the body is to be present with the Lord." Those are the words of the Apostle Paul. (II Corinthians 5:8)This is the good news! It is so much comfort to us in time of grief.

FIND WAYS TO HONOR YOUR LOVED ONE

One of the ways you can deal with your grief in a positive way is to find ways to honor and remember your departed loved one. Payne Stewart, the professional golfer lost his dad to cancer. He was very close to his dad. Some months later he won a professional golf tournament and the prize was $108,000. He gave his entire winnings to an organization that helped families that were dealing with the trauma of cancer. This was his way of honoring his dad and helping others in pain in the process.

There are many ways you can honor your loved one. What did your loved one love? What were some of her major interests? One mother sent a girl to camp in honor of her own daughter. There are many charitable causes that you can give to that can honor those that have left us behind. One could even set up a trust fund and the interest could be used for worthy causes. Scholarships can be set up at one's favorite college or university or even one's high school. When you do things in memory of the one that you have lost, you help heal the pain of grief.

The Tennessee Valley Authority changed the life of a lot of people when dams were built to create electricity for thousands of people. Many people were required to move as the land where they lived would be covered with water. The story is told of one dilapidated log homestead that had to be abandoned to make room for the lake behind the dam. A new home on the hillside had already been built for the cabin's poor Appalachian family, but they refused to move into it.

When the day of the flooding arrived and the bulldozers were brought in, the family brought out their shotguns and other weapons. No amount of legal brandishing or bulldozer meanacings would budge this family from their cabin.

Then someone from the TVA decided to try one last-ditch effort to end the stalemate. They called in a social worker to talk with the family and find out what their problem was. "We ain't goin' anywhere," the family told the social worker. "Nobody can make us. We're not budging, no matter how many threats you make or how rundown our lil' cabin may look to you."

The social worker pleaded, "Help me explain to the authorities why you won't move into your beautiful new home." "See that fire over there?" the father asked, pointing to a blazing fire in the primitive hearth of the cottage. "My grandpa built that fire over a hundred years ago," the man explained. "He never let it go out, for he had no matches and it was a long way to a neighbor's. My pa tended the fire, and since he died, I've tended it. None of us ever let it die. And I ain't a-goin' to move away now and let grandpa's fire go out!"

The social worker arranged for a large apple butter kettle to be delivered to the home. She explained to the family that they could scoop up the live coals from the fire and carry them to the new home, where they would then be poured out and fresh kindling added. In this way grandpa's fire would never to go out.

The family agreed to move from their shack in the hollow to a new home on the hillside, but not until they could take with them the fire of their ancestors. There is an important principle here. Our ancestors are not to be worshipped, but they are to be honored. Their labors should be remembered. We should find ways to "keep the fire going". It is not only a way of assuaging our grief, it is a very important part of the human story. Our children need to know something about their family history. It is up to us to see that this happens. As a part of your grief work, you might write down the life story of your deceased loved one. It will help you and it will help future generations. How much of the human story is lost because it is not written down. Two months before my Dad died, I started writing a overview of his life story. It comes to seventeen pages highlighting the main events of his life. I feel that this short document will help my children and grandchildren and future generations to know and remember my Dad. If you do not like to write, make a video and talk out the story or take a audio tape recorder and use it to tell the life story of your loved one.

MUSIC HELPS!

King Saul had his bouts with depression and paranoia. The shepherd boy, David, was known to be good at playing the harp. He was called in to calm the spirits within King Saul's heart and mind The Scripture says, "David would take his harp and play. Then relief would come to Saul; he would feel better, and the evil spirit would leave him." (I Samuel 16:23.)

For ages, people have known the healing therapy of music. I had a friend who lost his youngest son. He was devastated by grief. He gave me a video that had been real helpful to him. It was a video of scenes from nature, beautiful scenery that was backed up by beautiful music. This video had been a tremendous help to him in his grief.

Listening to music is healing. Singing can be healing too. I knew an elderly man who had met a lot of grief in his life. He would begin the day by spending an hour in Bible Study and prayer and then he would spend an hour with his hymnal, singing out loud the great hymns of faith. Let music inspire you and heal your spirits during this time of sorrow.

VISIT PLACES YOU HAVE SHARED

One wife I know was bereft of grief. Her husband had died while speaking behind the pulpit at their church. He died instantly of an heart attack. Some months later I asked her pastor how she was doing. He said she had never been back to church since her husband died. The pain of going back to the very place where her beloved husband died was too much. I went to her home and gave her my encouragement. I even asked her to go with me to that church and kneel there at that altar and ask God to heal the pain and hurt. She refused. Actually, she was delaying her grief and making it even harder on herself. We must remember, grief must be faced with great courage. We must do the things that are so hard to do. In fact, everything brings back memories and we would have to leave our homes and leave everything to get away from the memories. But would we really get away? No! The only way to heal the pain is to face the pain. There is healing by going back to places you have shared with your loved one. One widow I know went back to one of the favorite vacation spots she and her husband had shared. That was extremely difficult, but remember, the pain does not go away till we face it over and over. What place do you need to revisit and quietly meditate on the good memories of your loved one?

Many visit the grave of their loved one and there find peace and closure. Some even take this time to talk to their departed loved one. There is healing. There is an emphasis on the good memories of days gone by.

FIND STRENGTH IN GOD'S WORD

The Holy Scriptures are God's gift to human beings in grief. The Bible is made up of the history of God's people. It is filled with prose and poetry. It is many things, but most of all it designed to be a book of inspiration. The opposite of depression is inspiration. We can let God inspire us and speak to us and comfort us through the Holy Scriptures.

George Washington said, "It is impossible to govern the world rightly without God and the Bible." Daniel Webster said "If there is anything in my thoughts or style to commend--the credit is due to my parents for instilling in me an early love of Scripture. If we abide by the principles taught in the Bible, our country will go on prospering, but if we and our posterity neglect its instructions and authority, no man can tell how sudden a catastrophe might overwhelm us and bring all our glory into profound obscurity." Patrick Henry said, "The Bible is worth all other books combined that have ever been printed." James Russell once answered a critic of the Bible by saying: "When they can find anywhere on this earth a piece of ground ten feet square where womanhood is respected, where old age is reverence, where men an women live in decency and comfort and where human life is held in respect--and God's word and

Christianity have not been there first--then let him air his views."

Make time in your daily schedule to open up the Scriptures and listen with the ears of your heart and God will speak to you and comfort you. The twenty-third Psalm, the fourteenth chapter of the Gospel of John, the thirteenth and fifteenth chapter of First Corinthians...these are only a few passages that have inspired literally millions of people. Remember, you need God to get through this period of grief. He is the only One that can heal your grief.

The French mystic Fenelon wrote: "The winds of God are blowing, but we must hoist the sails." We hoist the sails when we make time daily to read the Holy Scriptures.

BADLY MISTAKEN!

In Jesus day, as in our day, there were people that did not believe in life after death. The Sadducees were a group that fell into that category. They tried to argue with Jesus. Jesus rebuked them saying, "Are you not in error because you do not know the Scriptures or the power of God? Now about the dead rising--have you not read in the book of Moses, in the account of the bush, how God said to him, 'I am the God of Abraham, the God of Isaac, and the God of Jacob'? He is not the God of the dead, but of the living. You are badly mistaken!" (Mark 12:,24,6-27)

When God spoke to Moses, Abraham, Isaac and Jacob had left this earth long before. God did not say "I was the God of Abraham, Isaac and Jacob." He said "I am...still am the God of Abraham, Isaac and Jacob". In other words, God is the God of the living and Abraham, Isaac and Jacob fall into that category.

Jesus said to them, "You are badly mistaken!" He came down strongly on the side of life eternal. Later Jesus said, "In my Father's house are many rooms. If it were not so I would have told you. I am going to prepare a place for you." (John 14:2)

Jesus was quite clear. If this life was all there is for us, Jesus had no reason to lie. He would have told us! This is the Good News. This is the Gospel. Let's not listen to those contemporary souls that would laugh at the thought of life eternal. They are not wiser than Jesus. They simply are mistaken! Henry Wadsworth Longfellow takes sides with Jesus in his poem, "Psalm of Life".

"Tell me not, in mournful numbers,

Life is but an empty dream!--

For the soul is dead that slumbers

And things are not what they seem.

Life is real! Life is earnest!

And the grave is not its goal.

Dust thou art, to dust returnest,

Was not spoken of the soul."

(*One Hundred and One Famous Poems*, p. 123)

SHARING YOUR GRIEF

I once asked a lady what had helped her the most in her grief recovery and she said "talk, talk, talk, talk." We must not bottle up our grief but with the right person and with the right group, we need to talk about our hurt. There is a magic here. When we verbalize our pain, it makes it more bearable.

First, start with your family, those that are grieving with you. You are not alone in your loss. Others share that with you. They were at the funeral home. They were at the grave side. They have been to your home. They have sent cards and flowers. They have phoned you. It is a comfort to know that you are not alone.

The famous missionary Doctor, Albert Schweitzer, once said, "We are all so much together, but we are all dying of loneliness." It is important that we have time alone, but it is equally important that we have the love and support of others.

Grief can sometimes heal broken relationships in a family. Are there family members you can talk to and listen to? They need to talk. You need to talk. Find the family members that will not lose patience with you and talk about your grief.

I wish it were not true, but there are many people in our life circle who are not good candidates for these types of conversations. Perhaps it is because they do not understand the depths of pain that you are now in. Or perhaps they are just not ready to deal with the inevitable subject of death.

Our culture runs from the subject through denial or through fantasizing it. My feelings are that we cannot really experience life fully if we are running from the subject of death. We must be able to talk about it. Find family members and friends that will talk and will listen.

You can reach out to old friends that have had a similar grief. You can talk to them. Ask them what helped them. Learn from them. You will meet new friends. You may be surprised by the people that come your way and offer you their friendship. Invite them over for coffee and cake. Take them up on their offer to talk. You will be tempted to feel that you are so alone. But if you will open your eyes, you will see that you are surrounded by people who are acquainted with grief. Helen Keller put it this way: "When it seems that our sorrow is too great to be borne, let us think of the great family of heavy-hearted into which our grief has given us entrance, and inevitably, we will feel about us their arms, their sympathy, their understanding."

Ecclesiastes 4: 9,10,12b has something very important here: "Two are better than one, because they have a good return for their work. If one falls down, his friend can help him up. But pity the man who falls and has no one to help him up! A cord of three strands is not quickly broken." Do not face your grief all alone. There will be loneliness in your grief. But do not build a wall around yourself and wall out the many people that might help you. Perhaps most of the loneliness that we have is self inflicted. We can choose to reach out and open up. We help ourselves when we do that and we help others.

Now it is important to reach out to family and friends and enter into private conversations with them. But you may have the opportunity to go farther, faster. I mean by that, find a group that is designed for grief recovery. You may have one in your church. You may even want to start one in your church. There is plenty of grief in every congregation. You may call your local hospital or talk to the chaplain at your hospital. Your pastor may know of such a group or you doctor. It is so helpful to be in a group that discusses the landscape of grief. You will feel a bonding with those that are facing many of the same emotional, spiritual and sometime financial issues that come with grief.

Then, see worship as a part of your grief therapy. Your congregation is made up of all ages of people. There you stay in touch with the cross section of "the land of the living". Young and old share the issues of faith and courage. As you open yourself to the message of Jesus Christ, you will find healing and help. Some people drop out of worship at this point. There is some pain involved if you have worshipped regularly with your spouse and now your spouse in no longer with you. But, this is true of everything you do! If you avoided the painful, you would do nothing and that would only increase and prolong the pain. See family, friends, support groups and your local congregation as a great network of support during this difficult time.

Someone has well said, "You will forget those that have laughed with you but you will never forget those that have cried with you."

THIS TOO SHALL PASS

Abraham Lincoln told the story of an eastern monarch who instructed his wise men to write a sentence to be always in view which would be true and appropriate in all circumstances and in all times. They presented him these words: "And this, too, shall pass away."

We must see this as more than a trite cliché. It is the truth! It is a truth that is mentioned in Psalm 30:5: "Weeping may remain for a night, but rejoicing comes in the morning." We know that grief lasts more than a night, but it is a fact of life, the days of deep sorrow pass in time. The haunting, nagging questions is "when am I going to feel better?" We don't know when. Healing is a quiet mystery that takes place within the deep recesses of our heart. We must keep our spirit of hopefulness alive in relation to our future.

Don Ian Smith in his book *The Open Gate* talks about hope:

"Many years ago I occasionally drove through the little town of Armstead, Montana. I have stopped there for lunch break at a small cafe. But now the town is gone; it is at the bottom of a large reservoir created by the Clark Canyon Dam. High above the town that once was, people enjoy fishing and boating, often unaware that there was ever a town in that area.

"After the decision was made to build the dam and long before the town was covered by water, it was interesting to observe what happened in the town. It simply died. No one painted a house or fixed a tumbled-down fence.

"No streets were repaired; no one bought property. No one planned for the future. The town did not drown when the water came to cover it. It had already died for want of hope. Any persons, group, or society is doomed if it loses its hope." (p. 16)

"This too shall pass" must be more than a empty cliché for you. It must be a grand statement of hope that is based on your faith and based on the experience of millions of people. We must fight the temptation to believe things will never be better. God is working right now to help you heal. You will make progress. It will be ever so slow.

Believe in your heart "this too shall pass."

THE HAVEN CALLED HOME

Bob Benson's poem "Laughter in the Walls" says: " I pass a lot of houses on my way home--some pretty, some expensive, some inviting--but my heart always skips a beat when I turn down the road and see my house nestled against the hill." (quoted by Shirley Dobson in article "Coming Home" Focus on the Family, November 2000. p. 6.)

In your grief, you will find comfort in your home, your familiar environment. Others might think that you are better to get out of the house and away from the alone times. They are wrong. You will find comfort from the solitude of the loving memories of home. You need to get out at times, but your grief time includes times alone. Home becomes more valuable. It becomes a safe haven with comfort to offer.

"Home"

"It takes a heap o'living in a house t' make it home,

A heap o' sun an' shadder, an' ye sometimes have t' roam

Afore ye really 'preciate the things ye lef' behind,

An' hunger for em somehow, with 'em allus on yer mind.

It don't make any differunce how rich ye get t' be,

How much yer chairs an' tables cost, how great yer luxury;

It ain't home t' ye, though it be the palace of a king,

Until somehow yer soul is sorto' wrapped 'round everything.

Home ain't a place that gold can buy or get up in a minute;

Afore it's home there's got t' be a heap o' livin' in it;

Within the walls there's got t' be some babies born, and then'

Right there ye've got t' bring 'em up t' women good, an' men;

And gradjerly, as time goes on, ye find ye wouldn't part

With anything they ever used--they're grown into yer heart:

The old high chairs, the playthings, too, the' little shoes they wore

Ye hoard; an' if ye could ye'd keep the thumb-marks on the door.

Ye've go t' weep t' make it home, ye've got t' sit and sigh

An' watch beside a loved one's bed, an' know That Death is nigh;

An' in the stillness o' the night t' see Death's angel come,

An' close th eyes o' her that smiled an' leave her sweet voice dumb.

For these are scenes that grip the heart an' when yer tears are dried,

Ye find the home is dearer than it was, an' sanctified;

An' tuggin' at ye always are the pleasant memories

O' her that was an' is no more--ye can't escape from these.

Ye've got t' sing an' dance fer years, ye've got t' romp and play,

An' learn t' love the things ye have by usin' em
each day;

Even the roses 'round the porch must blossom
year by year

Afore they come a part o' ye, suggestin'
someone dear

Who used t' love 'em long ago, an' trained 'em
jes' t' run

The way they do, so's they would get the early
mornin' sun;

Ye've got t' love each brick an' stone from
cellar up t' dome:

It takes a heap o' livin' in a house t' make it
home."

Edgar A. Guest,

(Cf. One Hundred and One Famous Poems, 152f.)

EXTREME GRIEF AND THE ANSWER

In the Gospel of Mark (5:1-20) there is a story that comes out of the life of our Lord. It seems rather extreme and exaggerated but sometimes grief is exaggerated. You can be certain that there are those that are handling their grief with a lot less success than you are.

Jesus came upon a man "with an unclean spirit; who lived among the tombs". He was out of control. Often others had tried to control him by tying him up in chains, but he broke the chains. Night and day he was crying and cutting himself with stones.

What was this man's problem? We can only guess that he was insane with grief. He was living in the grave yard. He was isolated from everyone else. No one else could help him. He was constantly hurting himself, cutting himself. Today, this man would be institutionalized. We would call him "psychotic." It doesn't matter what we call him, he was a man whose life was out of control. No one had the answer for this man.

Read the story and you will see that when Jesus came upon this man, the man ran and worshipped him. He cried out with a loud voice, and said, "What have I to do with you Jesus, thou Son of the most high God? I beg you by God, that you torment me not." He recognized Jesus for who He was but at the same time He feared that Jesus was going to torment him!

Are there many people today that feel that God has forsaken them and has nothing good for them. Some even see their grief as a punishment from God and the taking of one's loved one is God's way of punishing the one in grief. It is an important question: Does Jesus help us or hurt us? Is He wanting to punish you, or to help you in the most profound way?

Jesus asked the man, "What is your name?" The man said, "My name is Legion: for we are many." This was a strange answer. A legion is an army. In the Roman army, a legion consisted of 3,000-6000 infantry troops and 100-200 cavalry troops. What did this man mean when he said his name was Legion? Our modern psychology would say this means he was a divided person with different personalities and different identities. He was one person now and another person later. He was good and bad, weak and strong, sane and insane. He was confused about who he was.

Spiritual warfare is more than just a theological theory. It is going on all the time. There are forces of good that would build us up and there are forces of evil that would tear us down. When we are in grief, we can feel so helpless and we can feel that we will never be normal again. One widow, a year after the loss of her husband said to me, "When you lose your mate, you feel like half your body just doesn't function."

Now Jesus said to the man, "Come out of the man, you unclean spirit". The unclean spirit was exorcised. And the story goes on to say that the neighbors were shocked to find the man "clothed and in his right mind". I hardly think there is a more beautiful picture in all of the sacred scriptures of the healing, saving, changing power of God than we find right here. "In his right mind". That is God's will for you. He has not come to condemn you, but to save you and to help you. He is the answer that you can not find anywhere else. Others try to help, but your most profound help will come from Jesus Christ as you turn to him in child like faith. And then day by day walk in the power of His grace.

Sometimes we cannot get the message. We have to talk to a trusted friend. Find the right person. It might be a pastor. It may be a Christian leader whom you look up to. Open your heart to that person and they too can be instruments of God's grace and help you to know that God is for you and not against you.

LOOK AT THE BIG PICTURE

A man was walking by a construction site where a new church building was to be erected. He saw three workmen digging for the foundation. "What are you men doing?" he asked. One man answered, "I'm digging a hole." The second responded, "I'm earning a living". The third proudly said, "I'm helping to build a cathedral." We can take a different perspective on what we are doing. We can minimize our life and our work or we can see our life and the life of our loved ones in the perspective of greatness.

The Bible has a theme that runs throughout the Old Testament. The theme is to remember the Exodus. Remember how you were slaves. Remember how God worked to deliver His people. In the New Testament there is another theme of deliverance. Remember what Jesus did for you. He died on the cross. Remember that this is the kind of God you worship. He is in the deliverance business. And that means, he is in the business of delivering you from your grief and the pain of your sorrow. God is working. God is a God of purpose. Your loved one has not lived and died in vain. You are not here without a divine purpose. God has delivered you from many struggles and crises of the past. He will deliver you in this struggle. Trust Him. Give him time! He is working silently in your heart, even when you do not know it. We are saved by our faith. We walk by faith. We live by faith. We keep surrendering our burdens to the Lord. He will supply all of our needs and deliver us from every bondage and grief.

The French painter, Pierre Auguste Renoir, suffered from arthritis in later life. A friend once watched Renoir at work, seeing how he held the brush with his fingertips. He saw that each movement of the artist's hands caused him pain. The friend asked why he kept painting when the pain was so great. Renoir answered, "The pain passes, but the beauty remains." (Cf. *Freedom from Frustration,* Hardy R. Denham, Jr., p. 98)

That is our motivation. God is working. He is working to bring out the beauty in the life of our loved one who is now with the Lord. Good memories last. The chaff is blown away and the best remains. Good memories of our departed loved one will inspire us and others. And we must see our life in the same way. Let's get the big picture. There is pain, but it will pass. Beauty remains. This is a testimony to the power and purpose of God.

REMEMBER-LIFE IS SHORT

We do not know who made the following statement, but that statement has touched the hearts of many people over the years. Here it is:

> I shall pass through this world but once. Any good therefore that I can do, or any kindness that I can show to any human being, let me do it now. Let me not defer nor neglect it, for I shall not pass this way again.

The mistake of youth is the belief that one has a long time to live. If we have wisdom, we know in our hearts that life is short and can come to an end here on this earth at any time. Now this thought should not alarm us and leave us in a state of paralysis. Instead, it should motivate us to action.

A good question to ask is: why am I left behind? So many have died before us. Many have died that are younger than we are. Why are we left behind? As you answer that question you will be more in touch with your power and your purpose. You can do good. You can show kindness. You can do it everyday.

Anna Russell wrote a song about our ability to choose what we are going to do with the rest of our life. We can make excuses for nonliving, or we can choose to take responsibility for our future.

"I went to my psychiatrist to be psychoanalyzed,

To find out why I killed the cat and blackened my wife's eyes.

He put me on a downy couch to see what he could find,

And this is what he dredged up from my subconscious

mind:

When I was one, my mommy hid my dolly in the trunk,

And so it follows naturally, that I am always drunk.

When I was two, I saw my father kiss the maid one

day,

And that is why I suffer from ambivalence toward my brothers,

So it follows naturally, I poisoned all my lovers.

I'm so glad that I have learned the lesson it has taught,

That everything I do that's wrong is someone else's fault."

(Cf. Total Joy, Marabel Morgan, p 29f)

Your healing comes as you begin to take responsibility for your future. Ultimate freedom, according to Dr. Viktor E. Frankl, is man's right to choose his own attitude in a given set of circumstances. Your circumstances have been painful. You have been left behind. You have experienced loneliness and depression. It is so important that you choose the right attitude at this very pain filled time in your life.

An interview was done of people 65 and over, thousands of them, and only 20% of these people said they were "happy". The rest called themselves "victims." Is that where we're headed? Is that the point of life? We have a choice, to be in the 80% who feel like they are victims or to be in the 20% who are responding positively to what life brings. What is your choice?

Leo Buscaglia tells of an experience worth sharing. "I remember my dad being really despondent. And by the way, they never hid life from us. They always let us know when they were despondent, unhappy and fearful. They never let us believe they were Rocks of Gibraltar. They always let us know they were human, and for that I'm grateful. They were not symbols of perfection; they were symbols of humaness!

"I remember Dad sitting down and telling us that his partner had absconded with all the money and he didn't even know where our next meal was coming from. Mama had the craziest habit, she loved to laugh. And that just struck her funny. He was furious with her! She was laughing, tears were coming down her cheeks. You know what she did? We all went off and came home that evening and she had prepared a banquet such as we would have for a baptism, or a wedding: antipasto, pasta, veal, everything! My father said, "My God, what's this?' She said, 'I spent everything on this.' He said, 'You are crazy'. She said, 'The time we need joy is now, not later. This is the time to be happy. Shut up and eat!'"(Cf. *Living, Loving & Learning*, p. 166,173)

The Bible talks about the "land of the living". It is God's will that we have an abundant life as opposed to being victims with only a gloomy existence. The early Church Father, Irenaeus once said, "The glory of God is a man/woman fully alive". God's greatest thrill is seeing his people living life fully. Now all this must take place in a world where there is grief and pain. But we can choose life everyday.

Buscaglia goes on with some helpful comments in this area. "We have to make peace with our death in order to choose life, because death is an incredibly good friend. It tells us that we don't have forever. And if you want life, you'd better live it now! Because if you wait, it may not be there. A wonderful thing about Democratic Death is that nobody knows when it's coming. And so it's a challenge to you to live every moment as if death were sitting saying to you, 'I'm here, I'm here!' There's nothing more abhorrent to us in our culture than a concept of death. I have never seen a people more afraid of death than in the United States. You know why? Because we don't live! If we lived, we would not fear death.

"If you lived every moment--every God-given moment--when your time came, you wouldn't be screaming and yelling. Ask people who are studying death who the people are who die happily. It's those people who attempted to know life." (pp. 180f)

The famous painter, Van Gogh gives us a secret in this important choice of choosing life. He said, "The best way to love life is to love many things." What are your interests? What sparks our curiosity and what are the things that you enjoy.

There is music, there is the world of art, there is the world of computers, there is the world of education. There is the world of poetry and literature. There is the world of personal friendships. There is the world of faith and inspiration. There is the world of food and sports. There is the world of plants and the world of animals. God has given us a world that is full of ways for us to turn on our passions. Each person is different here. Find what really thrills you and follow that passion as well as others. Life is short. That is our motivation for choosing life now.

THE DAFFODIL PRINCIPLE

A mother tells of her daughter telephoning to say, "Mother, you must come see the daffodils before they are over." She wanted to go, but it was a two-hour drive from Laguna to Lake Arrowhead. "I will come next Tuesday, " she promised, a little reluctantly on her third call. "

The next Tuesday was cold and rainy. She told her daughter, "Forget the daffodils, Carolyn! The road is invisible in the clouds and fog". Her daughter smiled calmly and said, "We drive in this all the time, Mother."

"Well, you won't get me back on the road until it clears, and then I'm heading for home!" I assured her.

"I was hoping you'd take me over to the garage to pick up my car." "How far will we have to drive?"

"Just a few blocks," Carolyn said. "I'll drive. I'm used to this."

After several minutes, the mother had to ask, "Where are we going? This isn't the way to the garage!"

"We're going to my garage the long way," Carolyn

smiled, "by way of the daffodils."

"Carolyn," her mother said sternly, "please turn around."

"It's all right, Mother, I promise. You will never forgive yourself if you miss this experience."

After about twenty minutes, they turned onto a small gravel road and they saw a small church. On the far side of the church, they saw a hand lettered sign that read, "Daffodil Garden"

They got out of the car and each took a child's hand, and mother followed daughter down the path. Then, they turned a corner of the path, and the mother looked up and gasped. Before her lay the most glorious sight. It looked as though someone had taken a great vat of gold and poured it down over the mountain peak and slopes. The flowers were planted in majestic, swirling patterns-great ribbons and swaths of deep orange, white, lemon yellow, salmon, pink, saffron, and butter yellow. Each different-colored variety was planted as a group so that it swirled and flowed like its own river with its own unique hue. There were five acres of flowers.

"But who has done this?" the mother asked. "It's just one woman," Carolyn answered. "She lives on the property. That's her home." Carolyn pointed to a well kept A-frame house that looked small and modest in the midst of all that glory.

They walked up to the house. On the patio, they saw a poster. "Answers to the Questions I Know You Are Asking" was the headline. The first answer was a simple one. It read,"50,000 bulbs". The second answer was, "One at a time, by one woman. Two hands, two feet, and very little brain." The third answer was, "Began in 1958."

There it was, "The Daffodil Principle". The mother said, "That moment was a life-changing experience. I thought of this woman whom I had never met, who, more than forty years before, had begun-one bulb at a time-to bring her vision of beauty and joy to an obscure mountain top. Still, just planting one bulb at a time, year after year, had changed the world. This unknown woman had forever changed the world in which she lived. She had created something of indescribable magnificence, beauty, and inspiration."

The principle her daffodil garden taught is one of the greatest principles of celebration. That is, learning to move toward our goals and desires one step at a time--often just one baby-step at a time--and learning to love the doing, learning to use the accumulation of time.

When we multiply tiny pieces of time with small increments of daily effort, we too will find we can accomplish magnificent things. We can change the world. We can start today. Not only can we make our world more beautiful, we can make our life more beautiful.

THE SERENITY PRAYER

I know a mother who lost her nineteen year old son in an accident. She was thrown into a most terrible time of grief. She got more involved in her church. She went to the YWCA to swim almost every day. She walked a lot. She said that one of the things that helped her most was to say the Serenity Prayer over and over.

> God give me the serenity to accept the things
> I cannot change,
> Grant me the courage to change the things I can,
> And give me wisdom to know the difference.

Acceptance is hard. Acceptance requires divine healing and strength. Acceptance requires a prayerful heart. George Matheson was the renowned blind preacher of Scotland. He referred to his blindness as his "thorn in the flesh". He learned to see his "thorn" as a friend. He learned to pray the following prayer:

"My God, I have never thanked thee for my thorn,

I have thanked thee a thousand times for my roses but

not once for my thorn.

I have been looking forward to a world where I shall

get compensation for my cross;

But I never thought of my cross as itself a present

glory.

Teach me the glory of my cross;

Teach me the value of my thorn!

Show me that I have climbed to thee by the path of

pain.

Show me that my tears have made my rainbows!"

(Cf. *Why Me Lord?* by Carl W. Berner, p. 94.)

YOUR FRIENDSHIPS WILL CHANGE

If you have lost your spouse, you must know that this is one of the hardest grief to endure. One of the ways it is so complicated is that not only have you lost your spouse, but some of your close friends will begin to exclude you. You have been a couple for some years. Now you are seen as a single person. Married couples will not know what to do with you. There are exceptions with this statement, but to add to your grief is the changing relationships that will take place with your established friends.

Why is this? Some people will just avoid you because they have not dealt with the subject of death and grief and they do not want to. Death is a subject to be avoided in our

70

culture. Funerals are shorter, and some times even being eliminated. Our culture is death denying and of course this adds to the neurosis of our time. "If we do not talk about it, it might go away." That is the mentality of many people of our day. Of course, their life cannot be fulfilling as they try to escape from reality.

Then others will avoid you as they just don't know what to say. They don't know what to talk about. If they do talk to you, they try never to depress you by talking about your grief. Actually that is the main thing you want to talk about.

The main solution to this problem is to see this as a normal happening and give more energy to making friendship with those that are widowed or acquainted with grief. Who is it that can understand you the best if it is not those that have lost their spouse too? In the church that I served there was a group of widows that got together three times a week to walk in the mall and then have lunch together. Another group of ladies went out to eat together every Sunday after worship. A widow I know made friends with another widow and they take vacation trips together and are traveling friends.

Your married friends may not spend as much time with you now. But the day may come when they are left behind and you can be there and say, "I understand".

THE HARD DAYS--HOLIDAYS

The holidays are ones that hit us hard when we have lost a loved one. And they come one after another. The days that are so difficult are birthdays, anniversaries, Thanksgiving, Christmas, Easter, Mothers Day, Fathers Day and the date our loved one died. We must get ready for these days and not just let them leave us devastated.

One lady went through a difficult divorce. This happened in the fall of the year and she was left in grief and sadness. Thanksgiving came and she experienced the worst

Thanksgiving of her life. The gladness was just completely drained out of the day and it seemed so long. It was horrible. So she decided she would never let that happen again.

Christmas came just a few weeks later and so she took action. She invited all of the single adults in her church to come to her house for Christmas. Each one was to bring a dish and if they had children, to bring them too. Christmas came and she had a house literally packed with people. There was plenty of food and the fellowship was precious. She had not only provided a better holiday celebration for herself, she had brightened the day for a lot of people.

As the big days come, do not make the mistake of having no plans. Do everything you can to avoid being alone with nothing to do but feel sorry for yourself. Family and friends need you and you need them. You cannot get rid of all the loneliness, but you can get rid of a whole lot of it!

HELP FROM THE INTERNET

If you have access to a personal computer, you have a whole library of resources at your disposal. There are literally dozens of web sites that are committed to helping people deal with their grief. There are chat groups and support groups that are available online. There are many books and articles that are available for reading on the subject of grief. Most of these web sites have specialized grief information. Grief in it's many forms are addressed. There is information and support groups for children, teens, and adults.

Some of the web sites that I have found are:

AARP with a Grief and Loss Department

GROWW---Grief Recovery Online

Beyond Indigo

GriefNet.org

Crisis, Grief & Healing with Tom Golden

Shiva

The Compassionate Friends (death of a child)

Grief, Inc

grief-recovery.com

There are many more than these. There is always more help than you will need! Isn't that a wonderful thought!

THE SIGNS OF RECOVERY

C.S. Lewis stands out as one of the most important Christian writers during the twentieth century. He was a bachelor most of his life but while in his fifties, he married Joy Davidman. Not many years later, she died of cancer. Lewis wrote about his experience with grief in a book entitled *A Grief Observed*. He said, "No one ever told me that grief felt so like fear. And no one told me about the laziness of grief. I loathe the slightest effort."

He goes on to say "grief still feels like fear. Perhaps, more strictly, like suspense. Or like waiting; just hanging about waiting for something to happen. It gives life a permanently provisional feeling. It doesn't seem worth starting anything. I can't settle down. I yawn, I fidget...Up till this I always had too little time. Now there is nothing but time. Almost pure time, empty successiveness." p. 39

Now here are the hopeful words! "Something quite unexpected has happened. It came this morning early. For various reason, not in themselves at all mysterious, my heart was lighter than it had been for many weeks...And suddenly at the very moment when, so far, I mourned her least, I remembered her best. It was as if the lifting of the sorrow removed a barrier...Why has no one told me these things? How easily I might have misjudged another man in the same situation? I might have said, 'He's got over it. He's forgotten his wife,' when the truth was 'He remembers her better *because* he has partly got over it." pp. 51f.

One of the fears, or could it be guilt, is that we might get over our grief and in doing so, forget our loved one. C. S.

73

Lewis is helpful here. We should not feel guilt when the pain begins to lift. For then the memories can be sweet and cherished with more joy and gratitude. We never get over our grief completely. We never forget our loved one. It is impossible. As the Scripture says in I Corinthians 13, "love never ends".

Perhaps the saddest funeral I ever conducted was that of a young mother and her six year old son who were killed by a drunk driver who ran a stop light. Her husband and an infant son survived the wreck.

I walked through the valley with this family. I made it a point to visit with the lady's mother every year on the anniversary of the accident. We talked about Carolyn and Bobby. It was such a tragic loss. I did this for seven years. On the eighth year, when I went by to visit, the mother said, "Oh, I had not thought about it." That was the first year that she had not remembered the date of the accident. This was good. She was healing. She was not forgetting her Carolyn and Bobby. She was just moving beyond the deep pain of grief.

Micah 7:8 says: 'Rejoice not against me, O mine enemy: when I fall, I shall arise; when I sit in darkness, the Lord shall be a light unto me." This is a great affirmation of faith that we must write on our hearts. Our greatest enemy is death and the grief it causes. We need to say: "When I fall, I shall arise. When I sit in the darkness of grief, the Lord shall be a light unto me." Never give into the belief that you cannot go forward with your life and live again in spite of your loss. You can do it. Millions have! Albert Camus once put it this way, "in the midst of winter, I finally learned that there was in me an invincible summer". You will find a hidden strength. You will find wisdom. You will find courage. Grief can leave you a better person. Ernest Hemmingway said, "The world breaks everyone, and afterward many are strong in the broken places." Let it happen!

REMEMBER JANE

The introduction of this book focused on a young widow by the name of Jane. She had lost her husband to cancer. Her grief was complicated with a great sense of guilt. She not only had lost her husband but had prayed that he die. She had uttered such a prayer in times of anger when he would beat her while under the influence of drugs. Her prayer had been answered. Now she was flooded with guilt and was spending her days and nights at the cemetery and out walking the streets for miles at a time. What could I say to her that would be of help?

I decided right off that I was not going to tell her that she did not kill her husband. Everyone was telling her that and she was not accepting that effort to assuage her guilt. She *felt* guilty. So I decided to start from that point. I let her know that it was wrong to pray that her husband die. That is not the way to pray! She was guilty at that point. So now the question was "how do you get rid of guilt?" Of course this is a major human question as we all have our share. In every grief, our guilt comes up. We ask ourselves a million questions about how we could have treated the deceased better or we could have taken our loved one to another doctor or we could have done a hundred things differently. But it is no use. We cannot change the past. What do you do with guilt--real or imagined or a little of both?

It just so happened that I was talking to Jane on Maundy Thursday, the day before Good Friday which remembers the crucifixion of Jesus Christ. So I started talking to Jane about the crucifixion of Jesus Christ. I told her that Jesus took our sin and guilt on himself and paid the punishment that we deserve. Jane was punishing herself trying to remove the guilt. It would never work. We have a choice. We let Jesus take our guilt and punishment, or we punish ourselves throughout our life time.

So Jesus offers us forgiveness. He does not want us living a life burdened down by guilt. He does not want us to live a life clouded by the fear of dying. In His love for us, He died on that cross and prayed, "Father, forgive them for they know not what they do". Forgiveness is what God wants to give to you. His forgiveness is His way of wrapping his arms around you and letting you know that you are accepted. He takes the pain out of the past and helps you to move forward. Healing is the silent, patient, work of God in your heart. Wait upon the Lord. He has a brighter future for you...always! He is your Hope.

HOPE

Christopher Reeve is the well known actor that played "Superman" in the movies. He suffered paralysis from an accident falling from his horse. He has written a book entitled *Nothing Is Impossible*. He tells of taking a trip on a forty-eight foot sail boat years before his accident. They went from Connecticut to Bermuda. On the way they came into a storm that threatened to sink the ship. Here is what he says:

"The storm came from the north and reached us just before dark. We were sailing directly downwind with the mainsail and jib full out at right angles to the boat. The rain came first, then the following seas rose until they towered above us. Suddenly the wind gusted to 30 and 35 knots; all hands came on deck to take down the jib and put two reefs in the main. Even with the reduced sail area, we were now sledding down mountainous waves, the bow crashing into the troughs below as the storm turned into a full-blown gale. We weren't maintaining a course; we were just trying to survive.

"The gale pursued us through the night and into the following day. And then we saw the light. It was dim and distant; we could only see it when the boat was lifted on the crest of a wave. Every time we came up, all eyes strained to find it again through the blinding rain. Soon we realized that the light flashed for two seconds at ten second intervals. Someone went below to check the charts. Dead ahead of us, forty miles away, was Gibb's Hill Lighthouse at

Southampton, Bermuda.

"Light houses--tall, sturdy and built to withstand the pounding surf and raging winds--warn passing ships to avoid crashing into rocks or dangerous reefs near shore. Lighthouses have guided sailors through troubled waters for as long as anyone can remember. Seeing the lighthouse was like being held in the arms of a parent or a long lost friend. Now it didn't matter if our modern equipment failed. all we had to do was not lose sight of it and let nothing keep us from reaching its warm embrace.

"At some time, often when we least expect it, we all have to face overwhelming challenges. We are more troubled than we have ever been before; we may doubt that we have what it takes to endure. It is very tempting to give up, yet we have to find the will to keep going. The lighthouse is hope. Once we find it, we must cling to it with absolute determination. Hope must be as real, and built on the same solid foundation, as a lighthouse; in that way it is different from optimism or wishful thinking. When we have hope, we discover powers within ourselves we may have never known--the power to make sacrifices, to endure, to heal, and to love. Once we choose hope, everything is possible. We are all on this sea together. But the lighthouse is always there, ready to show us the way home."(pp. 174-176,2002, Random House, Inc. N.Y.)

Hope. Once we find it, we must cling to it with absolute determination. Jesus Christ is our Hope. He is the Lighthouse. Jesus said, "I am the light of the world. Whoever follows me will never walk in darkness, but will have the light of life." (John 8:12)As a sailor would have faith in a distant lighthouse and use that lighthouse as a safe guide, we are called to put our small faith in Jesus. He asks us to follow him. He is the Pathway through grief! He is the true way that leads to life. May you trust your grief to Him and follow him, day by day. He will be your greatest friend and your despair will be replaced by a faith that grows stronger day by day.

77

GRIEF PASSAGES FROM THE BOOK OF JOB

JOB 3:23-26 "Why is life given to a man whose way is hidden, whom God has hedged in? For sighing comes to me instead of food; my groans pour out like water. What I feared has come upon me; what I dreaded has happened to me. I have no peace, no quietness; I have no rest, but only turmoil."

Job 6:103 Then Job replied: "If only my anguish could be weighed and all my misery be placed on the scales! It would surely outweigh the sand of the seas-no wonder my words have been impetuous."

Job 7:3-4 So I have been allotted months of futility and nights of misery have been assigned to me. When I lie down I think, 'How long before I get up?' The night drags on, and I toss till dawn.

9:33-34 If only there were someone to arbitrate between us, to lay his hand upon us both, someone to remove God's rod from me, so that his terror would frighten me no more.-- Job asking for a mediator between him and God...pointing to Jesus.

13:4,5 (Speaking to his comforters): You are worthless physicians, all of you! If only you would be altogether silent! For you that would be wisdom.

13:15 Though he slay me, yet will I hope in him.

14:10-12 But man dies and is laid low; he breathes his last and is no more. As water disappears from the sea or a riverbed becomes parched and dry, so man lies down and does not rise; till the heavens are no more, men will not awake or be roused from their sleep.

16:2 I have heard many things like these; miserable comforters are you all!

16:15-16 My face is red with weeping, deep shadows ring my eyes; yet my hands have been free of violence and my prayer is pure.

17:1,7 My spirit is broken, my days are cut short, the grave awaits me. My eyes have grown dim with grief; my whole frame is but a shadow.

17:9 Nevertheless, the righteous will hold to their ways, and those with clean hands will grow stronger.

19:14 My kinsmen have gone away; my friends have forgotten me.

19:20 I am nothing but skin and bones.

19:25-27 I know that my Redeemer lives, and that in the end he will stand upon the earth. And after my skin has been destroyed, yet in my flesh I will see God; I myself will see him with my own eyes--I and not another. How my heart yearns within me!

23:10 But he knows the way that I take; when he has tested me, I will come forth as gold.

29:2-6 How I long for the months gone by, for the days when God watched over me, when his lamp shone upon my head and by his light I walked through darkness! Oh, for the days when I was in my prime, when God's intimate friendship blessed my house, when the Almighty was still with me and my children were around me, when my path was drenched with cream and the rock poured out for me streams of olive oil.

29:7-17 Job's deeds of righteousness

30:27 The churning inside me never stops; days of suffering confront me.

31:35 ("Oh, that I had someone to hear me!)

35:10 (Elihu) But no one says, 'Where is God my Maker who gives songs in the night?(cf. Psalm 42:8)

GRIEF PASSAGES FROM THE BOOK OF PSALMS

Psalms 4:4- In your anger do not sin; when you are on your beds search your hearts and be silent.

Psalms 6:6,7a I am worn out from groaning; all night long I flood my bed with weeping and drench my couch with tears. My eyes grow weak with sorrow...

Psalm 10:14 -But you, O God, do see trouble and grief; you consider it to take it in hand.

18:28,29 You, O Lord, keep my lamp burning; my God turns my darkness into light. With your help I can advance against a troop, with my God I can scale a wall.

22:14,15 I am poured out like water and all my bones are out of joint. My heart has turned to wax; It has melted away within me. My strength is dried up like a potsherd, and my tongue sticks to the roof of my mouth; you lay me in the dust of death.

27:14 Wait for the Lord; be strong and take heart and wait for the Lord.

30:5 For his anger lasts only a moment, but his favor lasts a lifetime; weeping may remain for a night, but rejoicing comes in the morning.

30:11 You turned my wailing into dancing; you removed my sackcloth and clothed me with joy.

31:5 Into your hands I commit my spirit; redeem me, O Lord, the God of truth.

31:9 Be merciful to me, O Lord, for I am in distress; my eyes grow weak with sorrow, my soul and my body with grief.

31:11 Because of all my enemies, I am the utter contempt of my neighbors; I am a dread to my friends--those who see me on the street flee from me.

32:7 You are my hiding place, you will protect me from trouble and surround me with songs of deliverance.

34:4 I sought the Lord, and he answered me; he delivered me from all my fears.

34:6,7 This poor man called, and the Lord heard him; he saved him out of all his troubles. The angel of the Lord encamps around those who fear him, and he delivers them.

34:18 The Lord is close to the brokenhearted and saves those who are crushed in spirit.

40:1-3 I waited patiently for the Lord; he turned to me and heard my cry. He lifted me out of the slimy pit, out of the mud and mire; he set my feet on a rock and gave me a firm place to stand. He put a new song in my mouth, a hymn of praise to our God. Many will see and fear and put their trust in the Lord.

42:3 My tears have been my food day and night, while men say to me all day long, "Where is your God?"

42:7 Deep calls to deep in the roar of your waterfalls; all your waves and breakers have swept over me.

46:1,10 God is our refuge and strength, an ever-present help in trouble...."Be still and know that I am God; I will be exalted among the nations, I will be exalted in the earth."

49:15 But God will redeem my life from the grave; he will surely take me to himself.

56:3,4 When I am afraid, I will trust in you. In God whose word I praise, in God I trust; I will not be afraid. What can mortal man do to me?

56:13 For You have delivered me from death and my feet from stumbling, that I may walk before God in the light of light.

57:1 Have mercy on me, O God, have mercy on me, for in you my soul takes refuge. I will take refuge in the shadow of your wings until the disaster has passed.

59:16 But I will sing of thy power; yea, I will sing aloud of thy mercy in the morning: for thou hast been my defense and refuge in the day of my trouble.

62:11,12 One thing God has spoken, two things have I heard: that you, O God, are strong, and that you, O Lord, are loving.

66:10,12B For you, O God, tested us; you refined us like silver. We went through fire and water but you brought us to a place of abundance.

73:21-25 When my heart was grieved and my spirit embittered, I was senseless and ignorant; I was a brute beast before you. You guide me with your counsel, and afterward you will take me into glory. Whom have I in heaven but you? And earth has nothing I desire besides you.

77:11 I will remember the deeds of the Lord; yes, I will remember your miracles of long ago. Keeping the big picture.

84:7 (describing those that go to worship at the temple) They go from strength to strength, till each appears before God in Zion.

86:13-For great is your love toward me; you have delivered me from the depths of the grave.

88:8,9 You have taken from me my closest friends and have made me repulsive to them. I am confined and cannot escape; my eyes are dim with grief.

90:12 (Life is short) Teach us to number our days aright, that we may gain a heart of wisdom.

91:11 (Angels) For he will command his angels concerning you to guard you in all your ways.

102:4,5 My heart is blighted and withered like grass; I forget to eat my food. Because of my loud groaning I am reduced to skin and bones.

116:3,4,8,9 The cords of death entangled me, the anguish of the grave came upon me; I was overcome by trouble and sorrow, Then I called on the name of the Lord: "O Lord, save me!" The Lord is gracious and righteous; our God is full of compassion. For you, O Lord have delivered my soul from death, my eyes from tears, my feet from stumbling, that

I may walk before the Lord in the land of the living.

116:15 Precious in the sight of the Lord is the death of his saints.

118:6 The Lord is with me; I will not be afraid. What can man do to me?

119:11 I have hidden your word in my heart that I might not sin against you.

119:28 My soul is weary with sorrow; strengthen me according to your word.

119:37 Turn my eyes away from worthless things; preserve my life according to your word.

119:105 Your word is a lamp to my feet and a light for my path.

121:2 My help comes from the Lord, the Maker of heaven and earth.

121:7,8 The Lord will keep you from all harm--he will watch over your life; the Lord will watch over your coming and going both now and forevermore.

122:1 I rejoiced with those who said to me, "Let us go to the house of the Lord."

126:5 Those who sow in tears will reap with songs of joy.

135:15-18 The idols of the nations are silver and gold, made by the hands of men. They have mouths, but cannot speak, eyes, but they cannot see; they have ears, but cannot hear, nor is there breath in their mouths. Those who make them will be like them, and so will all who trust in them.

139:23,24 Search me, O God, and know my heart; test me and know my anxious thoughts. See if there is any offensive way in me, and lead me in the way everlasting.

GRIEF PASSAGES FROM THE NEW TESTAMENT

Jesus said, "Blessed are those who mourn for they will be comforted." Matthew 5:4

Jesus said, "Ask and it will be given to you; seek and you will find; knock and the door will be opened to you. For everyone who asks receives; he who seeks finds, and to him who knocks, the door will be opened." Matthew 7:7-8

Jesus said, "Are not two sparrows sold for a penny? Yet not one of them will fall to the ground apart from the will of your Father. And even the very hairs of your head are all numbered. So don't be afraid; you are worth more than many sparrows." Matthew 10:29-31

Jesus said, "Come to me, all you who are weary and burdened, and I will give you rest. Take my yoke upon you and learn from me, for I am gentle and humble in heart, and you will find rest for your souls. For my yoke is easy and my burden is light." Matthew 11:28-30

Jesus said, " I tell you the truth, if you have faith as small as a mustard seed, you can say to this mountain, 'Move from here to there' and it will move. Nothing will be impossible for you." Matthew 17:22

Jesus said, "For where two or three come together in my name, there am I with them." Matthew 18:20

Jesus said, "Love the Lord your God with all your heart and with all your soul and with all your mind. This is the first and greatest commandment. And the second is like it: Love your neighbor as yourself. All the Law and the Prophets hang on these two commandments." Matthew 22:37-40

Ignoring what they said, Jesus told the synagogue ruler, "Don't be afraid; just believe." Mark 5:36

Jesus said, "Therefore I tell you, whatever you ask for in prayer, believe that you have received it, and it will be yours." Mark 11:24

Once, having been asked by the Pharisees when the kingdom of God would come, Jesus replied, "The kingdom of God does not come with your careful observation, nor will people say, 'Here it is,' or 'There it is,' because the kingdom of God is within you." Luke 17:20-21.

Jesus said, "He is not the God of the dead, but of the living, for to him all are alive." Luke 20:38

Jesus said, "For God so loved the world that he gave his one and only Son, that whoever believes in him shall not perish but have eternal life. For God did not send his Son into the world to condemn the world, but to save the world through him." John 3:16,17.

Jesus answered, "Everyone who drinks this water will be thirsty again, but whoever drinks the water I give him will never thirst. Indeed, the water I give him will become in him a spring of water welling up to eternal life." John 4:13-14.

Jesus said to them, "My Father is always at his work to this very day, and I, too, am working. For just as the Father raises the dead and gives them life, even so the Son gives life to whom he pleased to give it. I tell you the truth, whoever hears my word and believes him who sent me has eternal life and will not be condemned; he has crossed over from death to life." John 5: 17,21,24.

Jesus said, "For I have come down from heaven not to do my will but to do the will of him who sent me. And this is the will of him who sent me, that I shall lose none of all that he has given me, but raise them up at the last day. For my Father's will is that everyone who looks to the Son and believes in him shall have eternal life, and I will raise him up at the last day." John 6:38-40.

Jesus said, "I am the light of the world. Whoever follows me will never walk in darkness, but will have the light of life." John 8:12.

Jesus said, "If you hold to my teaching, you are really my disciples. Then you will know the truth, and the truth will set you free." John 8:3,32.

Jesus said, "I tell you the truth, if anyone keeps my word, he will never see death." John 8:51.

Jesus said, "I am the gate; whoever enters through me will be saved. He will come in and go out, and find pasture. The thief comes only to steal and kill and destroy. I have come that they may have life, and have it to the full." John 10:9,10.

Jesus said, "I am the good shepherd. The good shepherd lays down his life for the sheep. I am the good shepherd; I know my sheep and my sheep know me." John 10:11,14.

Jesus said, "My sheep listen to my voice; I know them, and they follow me. I give them eternal life, and they shall never perish; no one can snatch them out of my hand. My Father who has given them to me, is greater than all; no one can snatch them out of my Father's hand. I and the Father are one." John 10:27-30.

Jesus said, "I am the resurrection and the life. He who believes in me will live, even though he dies; and whoever lives and believes in me will never die." John 11:25,26.

Then Jesus cried out, "When a man believes in me, he does not believe in me only, but in the one who sent me. When he looks at me, he sees the one who sent me. I have come into the world as a light, so that no one who believes in me should stay in darkness." John 12:44-46.

Jesus said, "Do not let your hearts be troubled. Trust in God; trust also in me. In my Father's house are many rooms; if it were not so, I would have told you. I am going there to prepare a place for you And if I go and prepare a place for you, I will come back and take you to be with me that you also may be where I am." John 14:1-3

Jesus said, "And I will ask the Father, and he will give you another Counselor to be with you forever... the Spirit of truth...he lives with you and will be in you. I will not leave you as orphans; I will come to you." John 14:16,18.

Jesus said, "But the Counselor, the Holy Spirit, whom

the Father will send in my name, will teach you all things and will remind you of everything I have said to you. Peace I leave with you; my peace I give you. I do not give to you as the world gives. Do not let your hearts be troubled and do not be afraid." John 14:26-27.

Jesus said, "If a man remains in me and I in him, he will bear much fruit; apart from me you can do nothing." John 14:5

Jesus said, "This is to my Father's glory, that you bear much fruit, showing yourselves to be my disciples." John 15:8.

Therefore, since we have been justified through faith, we have peace with God through our Lord Jesus Christ. Romans 5:1

But God demonstrates his on love for us in this: While we were still sinners, Christ died for us. Romans 5:8

And if the Spirit of him who raised Jesus from the dead is living in you, he who raised Christ from the dead will also give life to your mortal bodies through his Spirit, who lives in you. Romans 8:10,11.

And we know that in all things God works for the good of those who love him who have been called according to his purpose. Romans 8:28

If God is for us, who can be against us? He who did not spare his own Son but gave him up for us all--how will he not also, along with him, graciously give us all things? Romans 8:31-32

Who shall separate us from the love of Christ? Shall trouble or hardship or persecution or famine or nakedness or danger or sword? As it is written: "For your sake we face death all day long; we are considered as sheep to be slaughtered." No, in all things we are more than conquerors through him who loved us. For I am convinced that neither death nor life, neither angels nor demons, neither the present nor the future, nor any powers, neither height nor depth, nor anything else in all creation, will be able to separate us from the love of God that is in Christ Jesus our Lord. Romans 8:35-39.

If you confess with your mouth, "Jesus is Lord," and believe in your heart that God raised him from the dead, you will be saved. For it is with your heart that you believe and are justified, and it is with your mouth that you confess and are saved. For there is no difference between Jew and Gentile--the same Lord is Lord of all and richly blesses all who call on him, for, "Everyone who calls on the name of the Lord will be saved." Romans 10:9,10,12-13.

But Christ has indeed been raised from the dead, the first fruits of those who have fallen asleep. For since death came through a man, the resurrection of the dead comes also through a man. For as in Adam all die, so in Christ all will be make alive. I Corinthians 15:20-22.

So will it be with the resurrection of the dead. The body that is sown is perishable, it is raised imperishable; it is sown in dishonor, it is raised in glory; it is sown in weakness, it is raised in power; it is sown a natural body, it is raised a spiritual body. I Corinthians 15:42-44.

I declare to you, brothers, that flesh and blood cannot inherit the kingdom of God, nor does the perishable inherit the imperishable. Listen, I tell you a mystery: We will not all sleep, but we will all be changed--in a flash, in the twinkling of an eye, at the last trumpet. For the trumpet will sound, and the dead will be raised imperishable, and we will be changed. For the perishable must clothe itself with the imperishable, and the mortal with immortality. When the perishable has been clothed with the imperishable, and the mortal with immortality, then the saying that is written will come true: "Death has been swallowed up in victory." Where, O death, is your victory? Where O death, is your sting? The sting of death is sin, and the power of sin is the law. But thanks be to God! He gives us the victory through our Lord Jesus Christ. Therefore, my dear brothers, stand firm. Let nothing move you. Always give yourselves fully to the work of the Lord, because you know that your labor in the Lord is not in vain. I Corinthians 15:50-58.

Praise be to the God and Father of our Lord Jesus Christ, the Father of compassion and the God of all comfort, who comforts us in all our troubles so that we can comfort those in any trouble with the comfort we ourselves have received from God. II Corinthians 1:3-4.

We do not want you to be uninformed, brothers, about the hardships we suffered in the province of Asia. We were under great pressure, far beyond our ability to endure, so that we despaired even of life. Indeed, in our hearts we felt the sentence of death. But this happened that we might not rely on ourselves but on God who raises the dead. He has delivered us from such a deadly peril, and he will deliver us. On him we have set our hope that he will continue to deliver us, as you help us by your prayers. II Corinthians 1:8-11

Therefore we do not lose heart. Though outwardly we are wasting away, yet inwardly we are being renewed day by day. For our light and momentary troubles are achieving for us an eternal glory that far outweighs them all. So we fix our eyes not on what is seen, but on what is unseen. For what is seen is temporary, but what is unseen is eternal. II Corinthians 4:16-18.

Therefore we are always confident and know that as long as we are at home in the body we are away from the Lord. We live by faith, not by sight. We are confident, I say, and would prefer to be away from the body and at home with the Lord. So we make it our goal to please him, whether we are at home in the body or away from it. For we must all appear before the judgment seat of Christ, that each one may receive what is due him for the things done while in the body, whether good or bad. II Corinthians 5:6-10

I have been crucified with Christ and I no longer live, but Christ lives in me. The life I live in the body, I live by faith in the Son of God, who loved me and gave himself for me.

Galatians 2:20

Now to him who is able to do immeasurably more than all we ask or imagine, according to his power that is at work within us, to him be glory in the church and in Christ Jesus throughout al generations, for ever and ever! Amen Ephesians 3:20-21.

But our citizenship is in heaven. And we eagerly await a Savior from there, the Lord Jesus Christ, who by the power that enables him to bring everything under his control, will transform our lowly bodies so that they will be like his glorious body. Philippians 3:20-21

Rejoice in the Lord always. I will say it again: Rejoice! Let your gentleness be evident to all. The Lord is near. Do not be anxious about anything, but in everything, by prayer and petition, with thanksgiving, present your requests to God. And the peace of God, which transcends all understanding, will guard your hearts and your minds in Christ Jesus. Philippians 4:4-7.

Brothers, we do not want you to be ignorant about those who fall asleep, or to grieve like the rest of men, who have no hope. We believe that Jesus died and rose again and so we believe that God will bring with Jesus those who have fallen asleep in him. For the Lord himself will come down from heaven, with a loud command, with the voice of the archangel and with the trumpet call of God, and the dead in Christ will rise first. After that, we who are still alive and are left will be caught up together with them in the clouds to meet the Lord in the air. And so we will be with the Lord forever. Therefore encourage each other with these words. I Thessalonians 4:13-14, 16-18.

In bringing many sons to glory, it was fitting that God, for whom and through whom everything exists, should make the author of their salvation perfect through suffering. Since the children have flesh and blood, he too shared in their humanity so that by his death he might destroy him who holds the power of death--that is, the devil--and free those who all their lives were held in slavery by their fear of death. Hebrews 2:10,14-15.

Therefore, since we have a great high priest who has gone through the heavens, Jesus the Son of God, let us hold firmly to the faith we profess. For we do not have a high priest who is unable to sympathize with our weaknesses, but we have one who has been tempted in every way, just as we are--yet without sin. Let us then approach the throne of grace with confidence, so that we may receive mercy and find grace to help us in our time of need. Hebrews 4:14-16.

REFERENCES

Barnette, Henlee. *Has God Called You?* pp. 109f.

Brothers, Joyce. *Widowed* .pp. 93,138.

Buscaglia, Leo F. *Living, Loving, & Learning.* New York: Fawcett Crest.

Cook, Roy J., ed. *One Hundred and One Famous Poems.* Chicago: The Reilly & Lee Co., 1958, p. 135.

Dunham, Jr., Hardy R. *Freedom From Frustration.*

Frankl, Viktor. *Man's Search for Meaning.* New York: Washington Square Press, 1966.

Johnson, Barbara. *Where Does a Mother Go to Resign?* Bloomington: Bethany House Publishers, 1979, p. 116.

Kupferman, Jeannette. *When The Crying's Done: A Journey Through Widowhood.* p. 95

Kushner, Harold S. *When Bad Things Happen to Good People.* New York: Schocken Books, 1981, pp.138, 191.

Larson, Bruce. *The Relational Revolution.*p.89

Lewis, C.S.*A Grief Observed.* New York: The Seabury Press, Inc. 1961, pp, 51-52.

Miller, Sally Downham. *Mourning and Dancing: A Memoir of Grief and Recovery.* Deerfield Beach: Health Communications, Inc., 1999, pp. 73ff.

Peale, Norman Vincent. *The Positive Principle.* p. 238

Prather, Hugh. *Notes To Myself.* Real People Press, 1970.

Reeve, Christopher. *Nothing Is Impossible.* New York: Random House, Inc., 2001, pp. 174-176.

Smith, Don Ian. *The Open Gate.* Broadman Press.

Stearns, Ann Kaiser. *Living Through Personal Crisis.* New York: Ballantine Books, 1984, p.65.

The Holy Bible: New International Version. Grand Rapids: The Zondervan Corporation, 1986.

Watson, Lillian Eichler. *Light From Many Lamps.* New York: Simon and Schuster, 1976, pp. 233-234,

Weatherhead, Leslie D. *The Will of God.* Nashville: Abingdon Press, 1944.

CPSIA information can be obtained at www.ICGtesting.com
Printed in the USA
LVOW12s1940260214

375275LV00019B/818/A